LORD'S ARMY
BASIC TRAINING

LORD'S ARMY
BASIC TRAINING:
A Survival Guide to the Christian Faith

Skip Wilson

LORD'S ARMY BASIC TRAINING

ISBN: 978-1-69412-416-6

This book is dedicated to my amazing wife, Kristin Wilson. The one whom the Lord used to bring me to church, the one whom I am always excited to see, the one who is my absolute best friend, my high school sweetheart and the one who I always want by my side. She is the one who encourages me, enables me and the one that has been used to make my life a tremendously joyous one. Of the many enjoyments and blessings in my life, she is the greatest next only to Christ Himself.

CONTENTS

PREFACE

I was teaching a class on evangelism and apologetics at a very large church. The class was to last an entire semester. The first class was going to be a quick overview of the Christian faith and then we were going to move on to how to share that faith with others... we never made it past the material of the first class. While it was a happy accident, the reality was that the individuals in the class knew very little about the basic truths that make up the core historical and biblical Christian doctrines. The hunger and thirst of those students for truth was palpable. While many of them had been Christians for years, they struggled with concepts like the Trinity, how we got the Bible, etc.

A similar thing happened a few years later while I was teaching a Sunday school class for high-school students at a different congregation. It began to dawn on me that this was a pattern. The reality is that we live in a time and place where more than half of professing Christians do not even agree that Christianity is the one true religion.[1]

It is for these reasons that this book has been written. This book is intended to be a systematic theology, focused on the absolute core doctrines of the Christian faith. The goal is not be original or particularly clever at any point. It is my sincere intention that virtually every statement and claim in this work be supported by a few thousand years of Church history and supremely supported by direct and specific Scriptures.

The goal of this book is to provide a firm foundation upon which one can continue to build a strong Christian walk. The goal is not to absolutely and completely cover every single possible topic. Through the many versions and revisions of this book that I have put together, I continuously think of things that I would like to add. However, this work is intended to place the primary focus on those Truths which are clearly mandated by Scripture and on Truths that are frequently misrepresented by the world and the cults.

Overall, the goal of this work is to give you a firm understanding of the Christian faith and how you can grow. Rather than seeking to answer every question, this book seeks to provide you all the available tools you would need so that you can find the answer to any question or address any situation. Furthermore, this book is written under the assumption that the bulk of the readership is at least a professing Christian. While the Gospel is clearly presented in this book, the marketing and title were intentionally chosen to appeal to a Christian target audience.

---

[1] According to Ligonier Ministries' State of Theology from 2018, 51% of professing evangelical Christians agree with the statement "God accepts the worship of all religions, including Christianity, Judaism, and Islam." https://thestateoftheology.com/

Some topics within the Christian faith are absolute and some are not. The mode of Baptism, for example, is something that must be inferred from Scripture as there is no clear verse that says that only one mode is acceptable.[2] The deity of Christ, by contrast, is unconditional as Jesus Himself said "for unless you believe that I am He, you will die in your sins."[3] The goal of this work is to focus on those things which are absolute.

It should also be mentioned that this work is not intended to be objective. It is the work of a Christian ministry (LordsArmy.org). When it comes to worldview, objectivity is an allusive myth anyway. The atheist views things through a naturalistic worldview, the agnostic through post-modernism, etc. This is written and built upon the premise that God has spoken through His revealed work of the Old and New Testament. However, while this book is not pretending to be objective, it is written with the sincerest goal of honesty. As the sheer number of reference notes on each page indicates, every effort was made to ensure that the Truths contained in this work are indeed Truths in accord with the Bible, Church history and science, logic and reason.

With the goal of truth and transparency in mind, the decision was made to put the footnotes on the same page as the content rather than at the end. In this way, the information presented can be backed up, challenged and engaged with more easily.

This book is written so that it can be used as a reference guide. To that end, each chapter is intended to stand on its own. While a reading of this book all the way through will provide a firm foundation of the whole Christian faith, each chapter may be read and understood to fully cover that one topic. Furthermore, each topic is

---

[2] The mode of Baptism specifically refers to the way in which one is baptized. The fact that a Christian should be baptized, however, is not inferred from Scripture but clearly mandated as in Acts 2:38.
[3] John 8:24, NASB

covered in each chapter from two angles. The majority of each chapter is written as the curriculum. The curriculum is the academic understanding of that topic which is broken out into subsections. The goal of the curriculum is to give a solid knowledge base of the topic. The final part of each chapter is written as the practicum. The practicum is the life application of the information contained within the curriculum. The practicum's goal is essentially to answer the "so what" question of each topic.

This book may also be used as a group study. A free printable group study companion guide is available online at lordsarmy.org/book that can help guide the conversation. The benefit of using this book as a part of a group study is that it puts everyone on the same page on those things which are critical to the Christian faith. Because of this, it can be a great way to kindly and lovingly correct many of the false assumptions of the world out there about Christianity. If you've ever wanted to start a Bible study group, you absolutely can. Nothing is more effective at making disciples (which you are commanded to do as part of the Great Commission[4]) than studying God's Word with another person. This book presents the Gospel, so it may be read and studied with believers and non-believers together.

This book also has a free, online and video-based course that you can access at lordsarmy.org/book that offers some further illustrations on many of the same topics as those covered in this book.

---

[4] Matthew 28:16-20

-1-
INTRODUCTION

Throughout the 1950's and 60's there was a man that became relatively well known for his many acts of charitable works. This man led a rather large church movement. He actively spoke out against the racism of the day; he and his people held massive food drives and did many good works. This church movement continued to grow until November 18, 1978 when more than 900 church members either committed suicide or were murdered at this man's request.[5]

This became known as the *Jonestown Massacre*. Jim Jones, the man that led the church, believed himself to be the ultimate fulfillment of the Bible. Using various verses of the Bible, he was able to convince many that he alone could offer them hope. Instead, what he ultimately offered them was poison-laced Kool-Aid[6] that was forced into the mouths of children and babies as their parents watched. Then, the parents drank it themselves.

---

[5] https://www.history.com/topics/crime/jonestown
[6] Technically he offered them Flavor Aid. However, the famous phrase "drink the Kool-Aid" comes directly from this incident.

Never, ever have any doubt. Theology matters.

Theology Matters

The horrible events of Jonestown are not alone. Jonestown became infamous because of the large-scale loss of earthly life, but make no mistake that there are thousands of false worldviews that are actively leading people to eternal destruction as we speak.

As Our Lord Jesus tells us, "Enter through the narrow gate; for the gate is wide and the way is broad that leads to destruction, and there are many who enter through it. For the gate is small and the way is narrow that leads to life, and there are few who find it."[7]

It is important to remember that the wide gate is not marked "Gate of Destruction." We can have no doubt that both the people going through the wide gate and the people going through the narrow gate are both thinking that they are headed towards the city. One way, however, the widest way, leads to a tragic end.

When Satan tempted Our Lord in the wilderness, Satan misused Bible verses in order to do that. To combat this, Our Lord responded to and defeated Satan by properly quoting Scripture.[8]

Prior to the Civil War, many individuals misused Bible verses in order to justify the American slave trade. By pulling verses out of context and ignoring clear Biblical principles, the slave trade continued. At the same time, however, it was none other than Bible

---

[7] Matthew 7: 12-14, NASB
[8] Matthew 4:1-11

believing Christians that ultimately defeated and dismantled the institution pushing for slavery abolition.[9]

Starting during the week of Easter in 1994, a one-hundred-day genocide resulted in the slaughtering of more than 800,000 men, women and children in Rwanda. A major factor in this genocide was a misinterpretation of the story of one of Noah's sons in Genesis 9: 18-27.[10] Although a wrong understanding of just a few Bible verses heavily contributed to the killings, it has been largely Christian non-governmental organizations that are helping to rebuild the country.

The reality is that human beings are made with a need to worship and serve something.[11] For some, they are a slave to nothing other than their own vices. The atheistic hedonist, for example, serves nothing more than his or her own momentary desires. As the writer of Ecclesiastes found out, there is no happiness in that worldview. The writer is the wisest, richest and most powerful person of his day, and yet he laments life saying "Vanity of vanities! All is vanity."[12]

Many people recognize that they are indeed meant to serve something higher than themselves. Unfortunately, idolatry is very common. Idolatry is simply the creation of and worship of any person, place or thing other than the one true God.[13] In his preeminent work, *The City of God*, Saint Augustine describes two different cities. The first city, the City of God, was created when all of creation was formed. The second city, the City of Man, was formed once Adam and Eve rebelled against God. "We see then that the two cities were created by two kinds of love: the [City of Man] was created

---

[9] https://www.thegospelcoalition.org/article/how-and-why-did-some-christians-defend-slavery/

[10] *The Curse of Ham: How Bad Scripture Interpretation Inspired Genocide*, International Mission Board. https://www.imb.org/2018/06/12/the-curse-of-ham-genocide/

[11] Romans 6:16-18

[12] Ecclesiastes 1:2, NASB

[13] Psalm 135:15-18

7

by self-love reaching the point of contempt for God, the [City of God] by the love of God carried as far as contempt of self."[14]

There is nothing more dangerous than the religious residents of the City of Man. These are the people who develop their own harsh religious traditions and/or use Bible verses out of context to commit acts of great evil. They form religions that are more about self than service. Hatred, anger, lust, self-righteousness; these are the fruits of the religions created by humanity.[15] Whereas the atheistic hedonist destroys only himself or herself, the religious zealots of the City of Man seek the destruction of others. Perhaps worst yet, many of these individuals are not even aware that they fall into this camp. Remember, both the wide and the narrow gates appear as if they are headed into the city.

The Battlefield

How is it that Christianity was used both to justify slavery and, ultimately, to end slavery? How is it that words like "Bible," "Jesus," "Heaven," etc. are used by dangerous and predatory cults to grow membership every day, and yet it is Christianity that is often the driving force to pull individuals out of those cults? Answering these questions is crucial for you to live a Christian life on this fallen world.

You are in a war. There are those who would like to see your destruction, and if you are a Christian, then there are those who would like to use you to defame and mar your King. You are a soldier in the Lord's Army, and like any good soldier, you must be equipped for the battle.

---

[14] "What did Augustine mean by 'Earthly City'", Justin Taylor. The Gospel Coalition. https://www.thegospelcoalition.org/blogs/justin-taylor/what-did-augustine-mean-by-earthly-city/

[15] Galatians 5:19-21

Thankfully, your King has fully prepared you for the battles of this life. He has given you internal tools such as the ability to use knowledge, logic and reason.[16] He has given you the Church and teachers to help guide and instruct you.[17] To born-again Christians, He has given the Holy Spirit who will "guide you into all the truth."[18] Lastly, He has given you the very Word of God in the Bible so that you may be "equipped for every good work."[19]

Core to the Christian belief is that God has spoken. The revealed word of God is our ultimate tool for understanding core religious truths. In his letter to the Galatians, Paul warns that "there are some who are disturbing you and want to distort the gospel of Christ."[20] He exhorts the Galatians to remember the true teachings of the apostles and says that if any person or even an angle tells of anything contrary, then he/she/it is to be *accursed*.[21] The Bible is indeed the standard of Truth against which the other means of understanding your world must be tested.

Sometimes individuals claim to have exclusive access to truth. You can call this guruism, and it is the foundation of many cults. Whether motivated by financial greed and/or a hunger for power, it is not infrequent that a charismatic personality will begin to claim that they alone know the truths of this world. They are often happy to impart this truth to you in exchange for money and control over your life. In contrast, the Bible and the truths contained within are absolutely free and open to anyone and everyone. There is no single earthly institution that can accurately claim some secret knowledge about

---

[16] Proverbs 1:7, Psalm 19:2, Psalm 119:66, 1 Thessalonians 5:21-22, 1 John 4:1
[17] Colossians 3:16, 2 Timothy 2:2
[18] John 16:13, NASB. This fact is echoed in 1 Corinthians 2:10 and John 14:26.
[19] 2 Timothy 3:17, NASB
[20] Galatians 1:7, NASB
[21] Galatians 1:8-9

God or life that is only accessible in exchange for money, lusts or power.

Beware of equivocation. Equivocation occurs when familiar terms are used in an ambiguous way so as to completely distort the original meaning. For example, Jesus warned us that "many will come in My name, saying, 'I am the Christ,' and will mislead many."[22] It is a common tactic of cults to use Christian terms such as "Bible", "Jesus", "Heaven", etc. in an effort to legitimize their teachings.

In late March of 1997, 38 cult members took their own lives in San Diego at the request of a man who claimed that this was how they could enter through *Heaven's Gate*.[23] While this cult leader promised entrance into the "Kingdom of Heaven", the reality is that the heaven he espoused was another planet accessible by a spaceship that travels behind Hale-Bopp Comet.[24] Not all uses of biblical terms are indeed in line with biblical teaching.

Be Sober Minded

You are currently deployed into a fallen world. As a Christian, this world needs you. You battle "not against flesh and blood, but against the rulers, against the powers, against the world forces of this darkness, against the spiritual forces of wickedness in the heavenly places."[25] In other words, you battle against dark spiritual forces, not other humans. No human is ever your enemy. Instead, they are prisoners of war.

---

[22] Matthew 24:5, NASB
[23] Heaven's Gate Cult Members Found Dead, History.
https://www.history.com/this-day-in-history/heavens-gate-cult-members-found-dead
[24] Ibid.
[25] Ephesians 6:12, NASB

This world needs you to act as the active soldier that you are. The world needs you to fight the evil forces in this world through love. It is important that you understand the core doctrines of Christian theology not just for yourself, but also because you are needed by the world. The suffering out there need you to comfort them, care for them and teach them of the God who made them.

Let no one outdo you in love and service to others. When racism rears its ugly head, let the Christians be the first ones to speak out reminding everyone that there is only one race- the human race. When natural disasters strike, let the Christians be the first ones there with physical and emotional aide. When a single, solitary person is brought to tears, let a Christian be there with tissues and an ear to hear. Be a doer of good at all times.

The Holy Spirit will use a solid understanding of theology to produce these changes within you. When you love God more than you love yourself, you will have no problem inconveniencing yourself to help others. When you recognize every human as an image bearer of God, then it becomes impossible to ignore their needs. You were not created merely to amuse and entertain yourself until you eventually die. You were created for something far greater than that.

The world is suffering out there, and you hold the cure. Be a sober minded soldier. Learn the Christian faith and its core teachings, but more than that- pray that these truths make you more like Christ.

Join the battle that you are already in!

-2-
THE GRAND NARRATIVE

There is one unified story within the Bible; examining this one story tells us the amazing Truths about ourselves, why we were created and why this life is the way it is.

The Purpose of Everything

Imagine the greatest possible being. He is not comprised of parts or made from matter. He is non-temporal which means that He is completely outside of time and unaffected by it. He is infinite and unchanging in His being- He always *is*. He does not learn because He is infinite in wisdom. He is not just a good being, but rather He is goodness. In other words, we determine whether or not something is "good" by comparing it to Him; He is the standard. Likewise, He is not merely a being concerned with justice, but rather He is the standard from which we determine justice and truth. He is holiness; otherness.

He is a trinity; a single being with three distinct persons. Within Himself, His relationship amongst the three persons, He is love.

A being that creates is greater than one that does not, and so He does. A Creation with a purpose is greater than one without, and so His Creation has a purpose and it makes sense that this purpose would be the greatest possible purpose.

So, what is the greatest possible purpose this Being could give to His Creation? The answer is surprisingly simple. The greatest possible purpose this Creation can have is to seek to obtain perfection. Not only should this Creation seek to obtain perfection, but also it should enjoy perfection.

The next logical question is, what is perfection? Well, that's already been answered. The Greatest Possible Being is the very standard of goodness... so He is perfection.

If you play that all out logically then, the greatest possible purpose this Creation can have is to seek to glorify this being and enjoy Him forever.

And so, because any other purpose would be lesser, He sought to glorify Himself through Creation. This is the ultimate purpose for all creation, including each creature in it, even you.[26]

---

[26] The Westminster Shorter Catechism identifies the chief end of man as "to Glorify God and to enjoy Him forever;" and draws upon the following proof texts: Psalm 86; Isaiah 60:21; Romans 11:36; 1 Corinthians 6:20, 10:31; Revelation 4:11; Psalm 16:5-11; Psalm 144:15; Isaiah 12:2; Luke 2:10; Philippians 4:4; Revelation 21:3-4

A Disobedient Creature

Let's call this "greatest possible being" God. When using pronouns to refer to God, we'll use "He" because God refers to Himself as He.[27]

God creates a universe; a vast universe of infinite depth and complexity.[28] In that universe, He creates life on a single planet. Among that created life, He chose to place a creature that is created in His own image. As God's image bearer, this creature will have authority over the rest of creation. [29]

Also as a part of being an image bearer of God, this creature will be wise, loving and will even have both the ability and desire to create.

God places within His creation a single, simple instruction. He does this because a creature that willingly chooses to obey is greater than one that cannot disobey. He commanded that "from the tree of the knowledge of good and evil you shall not eat."[30] This creature, however, does not obey. After listening to the "tempter" twist God's command into something evil, Adam and Eve (the first of these creatures known as human) choose to disobey God and come to know good and evil for themselves.[31]

The penalty for disobeying God is death, which God specifically warns Adam about beforehand.[32] In Christianity, death never means the cessation of existence; it can best be understood to mean

---

[27] Scripture contains over 170 references to God as Father, the New Testament alone has nearly 900 verses that refer to God in the masculine form of Greek and Jesus Himself was a male referred to as King. https://www.gotquestions.org/God-male-female.html

[28] Psalm 19:1

[29] Genesis 1:26-28

[30] Genesis 2:17, NASB

[31] Genesis 2-3

[32] Genesis 2:17

"separation."[33] Because God is justice, Adam and Eve suffered death as promised. They, and all of creation, were separated from the immediate relationship they had with God in the initial creation. Because God is perfection, then a creation separated from Him is not perfect.

That concept is worth restating- a creation separated from the perfect Creator is not perfect. This is the world that we live in today; a world far from perfect. While the old beauty and perfection that was once known is still discernable, it is clear that this world is not as good as it could be. We are only able to know that because we are given a sense of what was lost and of what should be.

However, the good news is that God is not only justice, but also love, and so He did not leave humanity without hope.[34]

A Specific People

Every human following Adam continues to make evil choices, therefore mankind worsens. Relatively soon, mankind got to the point where every single thought and action was evil.[35] Mercifully, God chose a single family; the most righteous available, and He chose to flood the earth in order to save humanity. As mankind approached the brink of self-destruction, God mercifully chose to save a specific people.

While the Flood made things better, humanity still has the problem of being separated from the Creator and so each person continues to rebel. Moral autonomy caused each person to desire to

---

[33] https://www.gotquestions.org/Bible-death.html
[34] Genesis 3:15 is the ultimate sign of hope; provided to mankind even within the very section wherein the Fall of man occurs.
[35] Genesis 6:5

overthrow God. So, mankind banded together to build a tower as an attempt to physically reach heaven. To make such collective evil more difficult, God spread mankind throughout the world, and gave each people group distinct characteristics and languages. Although every single human of every single race bears the image of God, He knew that mankind is too divisive to look past differences in each other to work together again.[36]

With mankind spread across the earth, inevitably each people group began to worship gods of their own creation. After a great deal of time, God chose a specific people group to set apart from the rest of the world. He told a man named Abraham that the entire world would someday be blessed through his descendants.[37] God gave to this people a special revelation (the Bible); providing more knowledge than that which could be known about God just from nature alone. Eventually this people group would form a nation, and God would display His attributes through His nation and its laws. These laws made this nation different from the world around them. Within this nation, He established a physical place where mankind could once again commune with Him directly.[38]

The Good News

This nation, set apart through Abraham, repeatedly rebels against God despite their ability to worship Him closely. After multiple warnings; eventually God, in His justice, put His people into exile before bringing them back to their homeland. These chosen people of

---

[36] Genesis 11

[37] Genesis 17

[38] This is a summary of the events that take place throughout the remainder of the Pentateuch (Genesis-Deuteronomy). This section of the Old Testament is also referred to as "The Law."

God were given a special promise.[39] They were told that a righteous ruler was coming, the "Son of Man." It would be through this Savior's goodness and sufferings that they would not only have a restored relationship with God, but also they could be given a new and perfect heart that desired to please God.[40]

Amazingly, it turns out that this "Son of Man" is also the "Son of God." In the most glorifying Truth revealed, it turns out that the only being capable of living up to the perfect standard of the image of God is God Himself in the person of Jesus the Christ.[41] Fully God, the second person of the Trinity humbled Himself by taking on the physical flesh and life of a man. He alone lived a life that could be defined as perfectly obedient to the Father, and therefore He earned the reward of having lived in perfect righteousness. He freely gave up this reward, however, and instead took upon Himself the penalty owed by sinners. By His death, the wrath that those who are born-again in Christ deserve to pay themselves is paid for fully. Those in Christ deserve God's wrath, but Jesus paid their fine in full.[42] Furthermore, He was resurrected on the third day as the sign and seal that He has defeated death for those who are in Him.[43]

In doing this, every single wrong act goes fully punished. This is important because only in this way is God able to demonstrate both His justice and His love. No sin goes without punishment, but the difference between those who will go on to have everlasting life and those who will be finally cast out into torment is who pays the fine. For Christians, Jesus paid it all.

---

[39] This section is primarily a summary of "the Prophets."

[40] While this information is contained throughout "the Writings" and "the Prophets"; this particular promise and information is contained within Isaiah (i.e. Isaiah 53) and Jeremiah (i.e. Jeremiah 31:31-34).

[41] Our Lord alludes to this concept in Mark 10:18.

[42] This is a summary of the Gospels and the majority of the Epistles; specifically in reference to the Book of Hebrews.

[43] 1 Corinthians 15

The Church

The new relationship that mankind can have with God now is even greater than the one that Adam had.[44] Those in Christ have the righteousness of Christ added to their account and because of this the Holy Spirit can now dwell within Christians. The Holy Spirit is the third person of the Trinity, fully God. This means that God Himself literally takes up residence in your heart once you have been made new.

Previously, the Holy Spirit dwelt *among* God's chosen people, such as in the Temple. However, now that the Christian's account is made perfect, the Holy Spirit can dwell within the believer directly.[45] This causes the individual to act as an entirely new creation, which is described as being "born-again."

It is the work of the Holy Spirit that produces this change of heart. Due to the curse of Adam and his decedents, each person naturally desired his or her own sense of right and wrong. The Holy Spirit changes that in the Christian so that his or her desire is now perfect, which is to please God.[46]

This is the establishment of the Church. The Church is not an institution or a building; the Church is all of those who are sons/daughters of God by having been born-again and adopted into Christ. Someday, the Lord Jesus Christ will return, and at that time God will be glorified in His perfect and final judgment. Those that chose to rebel against Him and pay for their sins themselves will do so

---

[44] In his book, *Human Nature in its Fourfold State*, the Puritan Thomas Boston makes this point clear- that the highest of all states is the state of the "Glorified Man."

[45] Hebrews 10

[46] Ezekiel 36:26

for eternity, and yet for another group, the Church, they will be spared even though they do not deserve Him.[47]

The Glory of God

Through the saving of the Church, all three persons of God are glorified. The Father is glorified through the demonstration of His love in the sending of His Son and the calling of the Church, and through the demonstration of His justice in requiring all sins to be paid for in full. The Son is glorified through the demonstration of His love in humbling Himself to the point of being born within creation, and more so by being born into humble circumstances. The Son is even more glorified by His life of perfect obedience to the Father and willingness to suffer unto death for His Church. The Holy Spirit is glorified in the facilitation of the changing of the hard hearts of mankind, through the work of the special revelation of the Bible and through the continual drawing of the Church to become ever more like Christ Himself throughout their earthly lives.

This is the Grand Narrative- the ultimate story of history and the purpose of life itself. Absolutely everything in history and all of creation is logically explained by the existence of the greatest possible being:
- *Whereas* a being that creates is better than one that does not,
- *Whereas* glorifying Himself is the best possible purpose this creation could have,
- *Whereas* creating a creature in His image is better than having not done so,
- *Whereas* chosen obedience is better than having no option of disobedience,

---

[47] This is a summary of the General Epistles and the Book of the Revelation.

- *Whereas* a being that is just is better than one that is not,
- *Whereas* a being that sacrifices of Himself to save is better than one that does not,
- *Whereas* a being that both judges unrighteousness and shows mercy is better than one that does not,

Therefore God- the greatest possible being- has done all this.

If the greatest possible being existed, then we should expect to find exactly what we do see in the world around us. As His highest name (YHWH) makes very clear- "He Is."[48] Because He is, so is everything else.

Practicum

It should come as no surprise that putting the Grand Narrative of redemptive history into daily practice is what the Christian life is all about. If you've ever wondered what the Lord's will for your life is, then just look to 1 Thessalonians 5:14-18 (NASB):

We urge you, brethren, admonish the unruly, encourage the fainthearted, help the weak, be patient with everyone. See that no one repays another with evil for evil, but always seek after that which is good for one another and for all people. Rejoice always; pray without ceasing; in everything give thanks; for this is God's will for you in Christ Jesus.

This passage has some practical applications of what is called the two great commandments. These are to love the Lord with all your heart, and to love your neighbor as yourself.[49] If you love the God that created you and redeemed you, then you could not help but be filled with constant thankfulness toward Him.

---

[48] https://www.gotquestions.org/YHWH-tetragrammaton.html
[49] Matthew 22:36-40

If you believe in Him, then you cannot help but to constantly be in prayer to Him. After all, He is the creator of the whole universe and you can access Him directly! You could not help but to love other people, because each person is created in the image of God.

Furthermore, you cannot help but to be loving toward your fellow humans because you know that they are important to God. You would know better than to repay evil for evil because, after all, you know that God is the ultimate justifier. You would be patient with everyone because you recognize that you, yourself, are in a constant state of struggle. Impatience is rooted in self-righteousness, but the Grand Narrative of Creation makes it clear that you and I are not righteous ourselves. And you know from the Grand Narrative that you are to encourage those in need and help improve those that need improvement because your ultimate responsibility to them is to seek to glorify God through your relationship with that person.

When you compare the Grand Narrative of Christianity to the other false worldviews, you find that only the Christian narrative actually makes sense of the world around us.[50] If the Christian narrative is true, then we should find a world around us that is filled with a moral consciousness and yet also filled with much evil. We should find a special quality inherent to the human being; one that desires to do good and yet does great works of evil. We should find a natural world that is oddly hostile towards humanity, and yet humanity still flourishes. We should find other believers in Christ as well as a special joy that comes from joining together with them to worship the Lord.

---

[50] Dr. Peter Jones makes this point in an online course entitled "Only Two Religions" offered online by Ligonier Ministries.
https://www.ligonier.org/learn/series/only-two-religions/

We should find creation very similar to a beautiful castle ruin, wherein we are still able to see the beauty that once existed and what still could be, and yet we also see rot, decay and destruction.[51]

This is the Grand Narrative of the redemptive history, and it comes with the simple fact that you were created for the purpose of God's glory. You will either glorify Him as an example of His wrath and justice, or you will glorify Him as an example of His love and mercy.

---

[51] John Calvin, C.S. Lewis and Derek Thomas have all given similar word pictures to illustrate this same point.

-3-
NATURAL REVELATION

Knowing the fact that everything exists for the glory of God through the Grand Narrative, we can now begin to examine what can be known about this God through revealed Truths within nature.

General Revelation

There is a lot about God which is seen from the careful observation of His Creation. Romans 1:20 (NASB) says, "For since the creation of the world His invisible attributes, His eternal power and divine nature, have been clearly seen, being understood through what has been made, so that [the unrighteous] are without excuse."

What are the "invisible attributes" of God that are clearly revealed within nature?

First of all, modern science has shown that there was a point at which energy, matter and space were not.[52] In fact, as modern science has figured out, even time is something that is actually relative and dependent upon the material space of our universe.[53] From these facts we can gather quite a few pieces of information.

Beyond Limits

Since matter, even as basic as quark matter, cannot have existed in an eternal past, then it can be known just from observational science that the source of matter is non-material or non-physical.[54] Furthermore, since time and space are merely concepts derived from the interaction of matter and energy, this "first cause" must be non-spatial and non-temporal because the cause itself would be completely beyond time and space.

So let's convert these terms from physical terms to philosophical terms. Non-material/ non-natural is supernatural. Non-spatial becomes omnipresent, and non-temporal becomes eternal.

---

[52] As stated on page 64 of Senapati, M.R. (2006), Advanced Engineering Chemistry (New Delhi: Laxmi Publications), second edition. The Universe is an isolated or "closed" system because it by definition does not have any surroundings. And within a closed system, the 1st and 2nd Laws of Thermodynamics have shown that matter cannot be eternal nor can it create itself.

[53] Norton, John D. "Spacetime." Einstein for Everyone. University of Pittsburgh, 9 Feb. 2015. Web.
http://www.pitt.edu/~jdnorton/teaching/HPS_0410/chapters/spacetime/

[54] Theories like string theory and other multiverse propositions are not only untestable/unfalsifiable claims, but even more importantly, they still depend upon matter to operate... which of course does nothing but kick the can down the road. Causality necessitates a cause, and the cause cannot be material or natural without causing an illogical/infinite regress.

Fine-Tuned Universe

We can see from this universe that it seems incredibly fine-tuned for life. The mathematical odds of arriving upon life through unguided processes are statistically impossible. Furthermore, the universe contains complex-specific information systems. These are non-random components of information which must be arranged in a particular (specific) way in order to function. It is important to know these because systems of complex-specific information are not achievable by chance alone. This is due to the Law of Conservation of Information. This law shows that complex-specific information in an isolated system either decreases or stays the same.[55] In other words, chance and natural selection are only capable of reducing information, but not generating it. Therefore, information systems such as DNA and RNA must have originated from outside the isolated system prior to the system having become isolated. Even mathematics itself is nothing more than an information system which was not created by mankind, but simply discovered by us.

The improbability of the fine tuning of the Universe as well as the impossibility of information systems arising from natural sources alone means that the aforementioned supernatural, omnipresent and eternal something has a supreme intellect and personally cares for the Universe. This something must also be fully capable to affect change, which is omnipotence. Finally, a supreme intellect that is also omnipresent and non-temporal is logically all-knowing, or omniscient.

---

[55]Dembski, William A., Dr. "Intelligent Design as a Theory of Information." The American Scientific Affiliation. The Philosophy Page. http://www.asa3.org/ASA/PSCF/1997/PSCF9-97Dembski.html#32

The Conscience

Let's move from the physical world around us to the psychological world within our minds. We are all given that which we call a conscience. Conscience is Latin and means "with knowledge." All people are born with knowledge of objective morality. We know that lying, stealing, murdering are all wrong things. We are able to look at the atrocities that happen around our world, and we say to ourselves "that ought not be." Individuals such as William Wilberforce and Martin Luther King, Jr. both stood at great odds with the society of their day, and stood up for that which is right despite what the societal constructs around them dictated at the time.

Now, imagine if you met a man and he said, "I like it when it's rainy outside." You may disagree with the man, but you are able to recognize that his viewpoint is just as valid as your preference for sunny days. That is because preference for one bit of weather over another is a SUBJECTive issue. In other words, it is up to the individual subject to make a claim of malediction or benediction on that topic. However, if you a met a man and he said to you "I like torturing puppies to death." Then, you would recognize his stated pastime as the horribly evil thing that it is. You are able to discern that you do not simply prefer "not torturing puppies", but rather you recognize that the act of torturing puppies for fun is inherently wrong. This is known as OBJECTive because the merits of it are based upon the object at hand and not upon the subjects involved.

This bit of knowledge regarding objective morality actually means that an ultimate standard from which comparison can be made exists. To make this point clear, take a look at this image:

If I were to say that "this is an apple", then you'd go along with me because the image has resemblance to an actual apple. Now take a look at this image:

If I were to give this image and say "this is an apple", then you'd assume the publisher had put up the wrong picture here by accident. The reason is because you know what an apple looks like.

The same is true for morality. We are able to discern a morally good thing from a morally bad thing because there is a supreme morality or measure that we weigh things against. If one person were to say to another "you lied to me", the person in response is not likely to give a response of "who cares if I lie or not?", but rather the individual in response is far more likely to give some reason why the statement this person made was not a lie.[56]

The conclusion you should come to then is not that "Belief in God is required for doing good." That's simply not true- believers and nonbelievers do good and bad things all the time. Rather, the conclusion you should draw from this is that "God is required for doing good." The reason is because without an objective standard of

---

[56] C.S. Lewis is the standard from which I drew this argument. His essay "Man or Rabbit" as well as his book *Mere Christianity* are heavily influential on this segment of argumentation.

morality; there is not a standard of "good" by which things can be actually weighed.

From this thing we call conscience, which transcends all cultures and societies; we can logically conclude that there is an actual objective standard of good. Therefore, this standard in philosophical terms would be "omnibenevolent" or "infinitely-objectively good."

In conclusion, from nothing more than mere logical and scientific observation, it can be determined that there is an omnipresent, supernatural, eternal, personal,[57] omnipotent, omniscient, omnibenevolent something. And we Christians know Him as God.

Practicum

The most important Truth that can be derived from natural revelation is that there is indeed a God that will hold absolutely everyone morally accountable. Absolutely everyone is without excuse, no one- regardless of whether or not they have access to a Christian church or a Bible is able to claim ignorance as an excuse. He has made His law known to absolutely everyone that is mentally old enough and of sound mind enough to be morally culpable.

Since God exists, then we have an absolute moral obligation to our fellow humans to preach the Gospel of Jesus Christ to everyone we possibly can. There are many people struggling and hopeless, and you have knowledge of the cure! You are to preach the Gospel. No person will ever stand before God's throne in ignorance, and you have the

---

[57] The fact that the Universe is so clearly fine-tuned for life is a clear indication that the omniscient/omnipresent cause is actually a personal force as an intentional action requires some level of caring.

knowledge that could save others from eternal destruction. This gives you a moral imperative to share that Truth with them.[58]

Another practical application of the Truths revealed in Natural Revelation is that we, as Christians, should not be adverse to science and logic. There are many in modern history that seek to paint Christianity as being at odds with science or the scientific method. However, nothing could be further from the truth. The scientific method based upon inductive reasoning was actually developed by a Puritan named Francis Bacon.[59] Science is simply the Latin word for knowledge, and given that Scripture tells us that "the Lord gives wisdom; from His mouth come knowledge and understanding"[60] it's simply untrue that Christianity is at odds with science. However, as the next module makes clear, Special Revelation is of a higher authority than Natural Revelation.

Therefore, in conclusion, the revelations of nature affirm logic/reason, and science is actually a friend of the Christian. From just these tools alone we can verify that God is real, that all people know He is real, and that those in Christ have an obligation to share the Gospel in reason and in love to all people.[61]

---

[58] Romans 10:14-15

[59] Sir Francis Bacon, Novum Organum, by Lord Bacon, ed. by Joseph Devey, M.A. (New York: P.F. Collier, 1902).

[60] Proverbs 2:6 (NASB)

[61] A fact reaffirmed in Scripture in 1 Peter 3:15

-4-

SPECIAL REVELATION

While much can be known about God from nature, some of the glorious Truths of God have only been made known through a Special Revelation. This is the very Word of God written and recorded for us nearly two thousand years ago.

God has Spoken

God's Word, His Special Revelation, has always been the most volatile battleground. Even in the Garden, the serpent questioned the validity of the Word of God and he twisted the Word of God.[62] In a recent study, only 32% of professing Christians agree that the Bible is

---

[62] Genesis 3

100% accurate in what it teaches.[63] This is important because if the Bible is actually the Word of God, then it must be entirely accurate. If it is not, then it is safe to say that the Bible is not the Word of God.

To understand the attitude that many, at least in the western world, have about the Bible, it is important to understand some key recent milestones.

The Da Vinci Code was a fictional book that came out in April of 2003 and achieved phenomenal success by selling over 80 million copies, being turned into a series of movies, etc.[64] This book is an important one because it contained a false narrative of how we received the Canon of Scripture, but despite being a work of fiction, this narrative is now a pervasive one. The idea presented in the book is that the Emperor Constantine suppressed 80 different Gospels in favor of the 4 that we have today at the Council of Nicaea.

While it has gone on to take many different forms, variations of this narrative has become pervasive in pop culture despite having no actual basis in history.

Canonization

In the year 397A.D., at the Synod of Carthage, the 27 "Books" of the New Testament as we know them today were officially Canonized.[65] The term "Canon" is the Latin word for standard measurement, and so in this context, it means that it was not until this time that the Church made an official, unified ruling on the writings of God. The 350 year

---

[63] State of Theology Study, 2016. https://thestateoftheology.com/data-explorer/

[64] "New novel from Dan Brown due this fall". San Jose Mercury News. Retrieved 2011-01-04.

[65] https://www.gotquestions.org/Council-of-Carthage.html

difference between when the Church was formed and when the Bible was canonized is inconsequential. The books of the Bible were not canonized before this date because they did not have to do so prior to the time of this council.

The books that had been considered for inclusion that were ultimately rejected were 1 Clement, the Epistle of Barnabas, and the Didache. The reason for the rejection of these works was simple; each of these writings was not composed by an Apostle or an associate under the direct guidance of an Apostle. Likewise, there are five books that are included in our Bibles were only included after careful scrutiny. The five books heavily questioned were the Book of the Revelation of Jesus Christ, and the Epistles II John, III John, Jude and James.

The criteria used to determine God's Word rested upon three main questions. Was it written by an Apostle (i.e. Galatians) or directly with an Apostle (i.e. Luke/Acts)? Was it widely distributed? Was it consistent with what God has revealed?

In this way, writings such as 1 Clement were not included because they lacked apostolic authority, and writings such as the Gospel of Thomas (which was not even considered) would have been rejected because they only existed in certain sectarian groups, and therefore failed to be widely distributed and/or directly contradicted known Scripture.

By asking these questions and scrutinizing the books of the Bible in such an objective way, the Church was able to discern the actual Word of God. That is an important distinction to remember. The Church did not determine or dictate what the Bible contains, but rather they applied objective standards to uncover what God has revealed.

Without a Doubt

The Church's heavy scrutiny at the Synod of Carthage accounts for the inclusion of 5 Books of the New Testament, but what about the other 22? The short answer is that those were never in question.

The many modern false narratives that some outside influence just chose, at will, what was included in the New Testament can be disproven by history. If this were the case, then one should find an early Church that is heavily divided about what it considers to be Scripture. Early Church fathers from across the globe should vary widely in what they considered to be the Word of God. Instead, what you find is the exact opposite.

Here is just a sampling of some of those early Church fathers going all the way back to just after the time of the Apostles. Justin Martyr references the 4 Gospels, and the fact that the Church read them as Scripture in 150A.D.[66] Irenaeus of Lyons confirms the 4 Gospels in 180 A.D.[67] Origen of Alexandria (240 A.D.), Eusebius of Caesarea (332 A.D.) and Codex Vaticanus (325-350A.D.) all confirm 22 books[68] and Codex Sinaiticus (350 A.D.) contains the modern New Testament.[69]

Rather than finding a diverse and unharmonious usage of Scripture, historians actually find an early Church that is consistently in agreement. This is especially surprising given the fact that Christianity was an illegal religion throughout most of this era which prevented widespread communication among the Church.

---

[66] http://www.ntcanon.org/Justin_Martyr.shtml

[67] http://www.ntcanon.org/Irenaeus.shtml

[68] Aland, Kurt; Barbara Aland (1995). The Text of the New Testament: An Introduction to the Critical Editions and to the Theory and Practice of Modern Textual Criticism, trans. Erroll F. Rhodes. Grand Rapids, Michigan: William B. Eerdmans Publishing Company. p. 109.

[69] http://www.codexsinaiticus.org/en/

Of greatest importance is what the Bible says about itself, and the simple fact is that the New Testament considers itself Scripture, inspired by God. In 2 Peter 3:15-16, Peter states that Paul's writings are scripture. Paul quotes from Mark, Luke, and Moses in 1 Timothy 5:18 and calls them all scripture. Furthermore, Paul said of his own writing that his Colossian epistle was to be read and circulated in Colossians 4:16.

Supply Chain

It is important to know the history of how the Bible came to us because the Bible is the ultimate authority given to mankind to direct us how we are to live, and it is the inspired Word of God.

"All Scripture is inspired by God and profitable for teaching, for reproof, for correction, for training in righteousness; so that the man of God may be adequate, equipped for every good work."[70] The Bible is our supply chain, and so it should come as absolutely no surprise that our foes seek to cut off our supply chain. It is God's Word that we are to turn to when we need help, when we want to grow and learn, for any and all matters of faith, because it is complete and fully capable of equipping us for any battleground.

It is an effective weapon;[71] "[God's] word is what goes forth from [His] mouth; It will not return to [Him] empty, without accomplishing what [He] desire[s], And without succeeding in the matter for which [He] sent it."[72] It is sure and unchanging, as the Psalmist says "Forever, O LORD, Your word is settled in heaven."[73]

---

[70] 2 Timothy 3:16-17 (NASB)
[71] Paul describes it as the "Sword of the Spirit" in Ephesians 6:17.
[72] Isaiah 55:11 (NASB)
[73] Psalm 119:89 (NASB)

While much can be known about God from Creation, it is His inspired Word that is the highest and most sure source of knowledge.[74] Furthermore, Scripture is what God uses to grow us in our faith; "...faith comes by hearing and hearing by the Word of God."[75]

The fact is that God has spoken, and He has provided us everything we need to be fully equipped in all areas in this life. We are to study His Word and spend time there daily; otherwise we're cutting ourselves off from our own supply chain.

He Preserved His Word

In 1947 a young shepherd was wandering in search of a sheep that had gone astray from the flock when he came upon a cave in the side of a steep hill. He threw a rock into the cave and was startled to hear the sound of a shattering pot. What this young man had just discovered was one of the most historically significant discoveries in history, the Dead Sea Scrolls.[76] The scrolls contain approximately 230 biblical manuscripts, covering nearly every book of the Old Testament, that date back to over 300 years before Christ.[77]

The reason that the main focus of this section has been the New Testament is because the Old Testament is largely unchallenged today thanks to archeological findings such as the Dead Sea Scrolls.

---

[74] Logical conclusion of 2 Timothy 3:16-17
[75] Romans 10:17 (NASB)
[76] https://www.deadseascrolls.org.il/learn-about-the-scrolls/discovery-and-publication
[77] https://www.deadseascrolls.org.il/learn-about-the-scrolls/introduction

How then can we know that the New Testament we have today is the same as what the inspired authors wrote? The answer is a scientific discipline known as textual criticism. The basic principle behind textual criticism is that you can determine what the original documents said by comparing multiple ancient writings of the same passage with one another.[78]

For example, if one highly trained and committed scribe in one place makes a mistake in his copying, let's say that he was getting sleepy and accidentally missed a line, then his mistake becomes obvious when compared to the other copies of that same text. It is extremely unlikely that another highly trained scribe in another place is going to make the exact same mistake in the exact same place while copying. By comparing and contrasting the manuscripts, experts are able to identify what the original text actually said. The more original documents available to compare, the more confidence there is in the reliability of that document.

Homer's *Iliad*, for example, is one of the most well preserved writings we have from ancient history. We have 1,757 early Greek manuscripts of the *Illiad*.[79] Now, that number is impressive. In fact only one ancient writing surpasses it, the New Testament. We have 5,842 early Greek manuscripts, and that's just the Greek.[80] The Bible was translated into various languages early on in its history, and if you factor in the Latin versions, the Egyptian versions, etc. we have tens of thousands of early documents to compare our New Testament against.[81]

Furthermore, most Bible translations such as the ESV, NASB, etc. make it very clear if there is a passage that has significant textual

---

[78] https://www.gotquestions.org/textual-criticism.html
[79] Strobel, Lee, and Jane Vogel. The Case for Christ: a Journalist's Personal Investigation of the Evidence for Jesus. Zondervan, 2017.
[80] Ibid.
[81] Ibid.

variations in the manuscripts by notating the variations in the footer or in the margins.

God has preserved His Word.

Different Translations

Why are there so many different Bible versions in today's western world?

To answer this, it is important to know a little bit about the different types of translations used. The New Testament was written in Greek, and the Old Testament was mostly written in Hebrew. When these words are translated into English, there are times when the translators have to make a choice. Some translations paraphrase the original text, which can make things easier for very young readers to understand but it also adds in a layer of interpretation that may depart from the original meaning of the text. Other translations use a thought-for-thought translation. This too can make a text easier to understand the original intent of the author, but also again adds a layer of interpretation. Finally, there are word-for-word translations. These keep the original language in tact with the least amount of interpretation, but can be more difficult to read.[82]

The typical Christian home usually has a few different translations, which is ideal because there is not a single English translation of the original text that does not have its limitations. The important thing is to be aware of which translation you read and be conscious of the methodology used by those translators.

---

[82] http://www.chapter3min.org/wp-content/uploads/2017/08/types-of-bible-translations.jpg

All Scriptural quotations in this book are from the NASB, which uses a very high formal equivalence (fancy way of saying word-for-word) methodology and is therefore very near the original text.

It is imperative that you spend time in the Word. You can have full confidence that the Bible you hold in your hand today is the inspired Word of God. It is your supply line in the war that you are fighting every single day. Just as in all war, your enemy is going to seek in every way to cut off your supply chain. Be aware that this is the point of attack, and make sure that you keep yourself well nourished by using this resource.

Practicum

Since the Bible is so reliable, and so clear, then why are there so many denominations and interpretations of the Bible? If every Christian assembly is using the same playbook (the Bible), then why don't they all agree?

One key cause of these differences is that there are two main ideologies when it comes to how to read the Bible. There are liberal theologians and conservative theologians. Liberal and conservative is not a representation of political affiliation, but rather these terms denote two different ways of looking at a text.

A liberal Bible scholar views the Word of God as a collection of individual beliefs and thoughts about God throughout ancient history. The text is treated as allegorical rather than factual, and therefore the focus is upon how a text can be applied thematically to one's immediate life or circumstance.

The conservative view of the Bible, however, seeks to conserve the original author's intent. Rather than treating the Word of God as a loosely allegorical collection of thoughts and feelings; the conservative reader assumes the reality of the text and seeks to understand the Truths that the author intended to convey. Much in the same way that the astronomer studies the cosmos in order to derive factual truths, likewise the conservative Bible scholar seeks to study the text in order to derive factual truths that can then be applied in the life of the believer.[83]

This liberal and conservative distinction illustrates different hermeneutics. Hermeneutics is the way one reads the Bible. The reality is that Scripture itself is very clear that it is meant to be treated as specifically factual and authoritative. A light to your path is useless unless that light actively reflects the literal path.[84] Likewise, the Scriptures are hardly useful for reproof, teaching and correction, unless they contain factual information.[85]

Given that the Word of God is described as unchanging,[86] and that the believer is specifically told to do what the Word of God says,[87] and that the Word of God is described as true,[88] then the Bible is clearly intended to be read with a conservative hermeneutic wherein the author's original intent is your ultimate aim.

In order to accomplish this, remember 3 questions while reading the Bible.

- What is the immediate context?
    - In other words, what is happening in this chapter and/or this book? Many interpretation errors occur

---

[83] The impact that Charles Hodges' *Systematic Theology Volume I* had on this section cannot be understated.

[84] Psalm 119:105 w/ common sense applied.

[85] 2 Timothy 3:16-17

[86] Isaiah 40:8; Matthew 24:35

[87] James 1:22; Luke 11:28; Matthew 7:24

[88] Psalm 33:4; John 7:38

because a sentence is pulled out of a chapter and used in a completely different context. If you would not do that to another book, certainly don't do that to the Bible.

- What is the historical context?
    - Who is the author? Who is the immediate intended audience? When was this text written? What was the author's purpose in writing this text? All of these questions can help you understand what is actually being said. You live in a day and an age when this information is easier to come by than ever before- with the answer to these questions just being a single search away. Use that to your advantage to grow in understanding.

- Finally, what is the Scriptural context?
    - Given that all of Scripture is the inspired Word of God; know that it does not contradict itself. Interpret Scripture against Scripture, especially when studying a particular topic in order to understand the broad revealed Truths.

-5-
THE GOSPEL

When a great military battle came to a victorious end, the message of the victory would be told throughout the kingdom, from village to village so that the civilians of a society could share equally in the victory celebration. This was known as the *euangelion*, or good news. The Gospel is the great and ultimate good news.[89] The ultimate battle of mankind has been fought and our supreme enemy (death) has been defeated. This is the good news that we are to carry.

Moralism Gospel

Perhaps the most common misconception about the Gospel is that of moralism. Judging from the name alone, something like moralism

---

[89] Baker's Evangelical Dictionary of Biblical Theology.
https://www.biblestudytools.com/dictionaries/bakers-evangelical-dictionary/evangelize-evangelism.html

may sound like something that a Christian should embrace. After all, it's the Christians that are to be the moral preservationists in the fallen world. However, in reality, moralism is one of the most pervasive and prolific anti-Christian doctrines in our world today. So, what is moralism?

To put it simply, moralism is the teaching that the core of Christianity can be reduced to improvements in personal behavior.[90] It is the false notion that we can obtain righteousness through good deeds and better behavior. This type of teaching reduces the Bible into little more than a how-to book for life. If this doesn't seem like a big deal, then just think about what this teaching produces. The Moralism Gospel produces sinners that are potentially better behaved, but are ultimately still destined for an eternity in Hell.

This is the main problem with moralism; it distracts from the actual Gospel. As the Apostle Paul wrote, "by the works of the Law no flesh will be justified."[91] Moralism changes the overall focus of our lives from Christ to us. Rather than causing us to bow down before God, we are encouraged to "stand tall" and "get our act together." We are told to look inward to ourselves rather than upward to Christ.

Moralism is nothing new. Our Lord dealt with it directly in Matthew 19:16-26. In this passage, a rich young ruler asks Him what he must "do" to obtain everlasting life. The ruler addresses the teacher as "good" in his question as well. Our Lord first corrects this young man's concept of "good", saying that only God is good. Jesus then goes on to answer the question. What must a person "do" to inherit eternal life? Well, that's easy- just perfectly keep the commandments. The ruler sees no problem there, declaring brazenly

---

[90] This definition is a paraphrase of this the definition offered by Al Mohler's in his article, "Why Moralism is not the Gospel- And Why So Many Christians Think It Is. https://albertmohler.com/2009/09/03/why-moralism-is-not-the-gospel-and-why-so-many-christians-think-it-is/

[91] Galatians 2:16, NASB

that he's done that already (keep in mind that Our Lord has just reminded him that none is good but God). Then Jesus, seeing the man's heart, tells him to give up his possessions, and the man walks away in frustration and grief. The rich man wanted to earn righteousness for himself, but he of course was unwilling and unable to do so.

This is the second problem with moralism. It breeds frustration and actively turns individuals away from the God. Imagine train cars on a train track. A person can show the train cars where the tracks are all day long, but those train cars are not capable of moving themselves. They need an engine in order to move.[92] Telling a group of people not to lie, not to steal, not to lust, etc., is not likely to yield any eternal fruit. These are not bad things, just like it's not bad that a train stay on its train tracks. Indeed, a train must stay on its tracks and a person should not engage in those things. However, just like train cars cannot move without an engine- those individuals are not going to be saved without the Gospel. The Gospel is that engine.

Our Lord makes this point clear at the end of that passage about the rich young ruler. After discussing how hard it is for a rich person to let go of his/her wealth, the disciples begin to question who is able to be saved. "And looking at them Jesus said to them, 'With people this is impossible, but with God all things are possible.'"[93]

The Moralism Gospel is rampant in our modern culture. According to a study done in 2018, 66% of professing Christians in the United States at least somewhat agree that salvation is the product of one's own works rather than through Christ alone.[94] When more than half

---

[92] This train and train track example were directly taken from a short-film called *American Gospel: Christ Alone.*
https://www.youtube.com/watch?v=ocHm18wUAGU
[93] Matthew 19:26, NASB
[94] Ligonier Ministries' State of Theology, Statement 13, 2018.
https://thestateoftheology.com/data-

of professing Christians in a country embrace a known heresy, it's worth explaining thoroughly.

The Gospel is not the key to a better earthly life.[95] The Gospel is not about living a kinder, gentler life. The Gospel is not about overcoming addiction. The Gospel is so much greater than these trivial desires.

The Law

Now that moralism has been thoroughly refuted, let's talk about what role the Law does play in the Gospel. According to the Apostle Paul, "the Law has become our tutor to lead us to Christ, so that we may be justified by faith."[96] This is the primary use of the Law for us today; it is a mirror.[97]

Going back to the very beginning for a minute; we were created in God's image.[98] As God's image bearer within creation, God gave mankind authority over all of creation.[99] We are to display and honor His attributes and to represent Him perfectly on this earth.

This is why, when we sin, we are offending God directly. That is the reason why only God can forgive sins,[100] because He is the offended party. King David certainly understood this. David lusted after Bathsheba, ultimately committing adultery with her and having

---

explorer/2018/13?AGE=30&MF=14&REGION=30&EDUCATION=62&INCOME=254 &MARITAL=126&ETHNICITY=62&RELTRAD=62&ATTENDANCE=254

[95] Quite the opposite, the Gospel often brings earthly suffering: Philippians 3:10, 1 Peter 4:13, 2 Corinthians 13:4, 2 Corinthians 1:5, etc.

[96] Galatians 3:24, NASB

[97] James uses this same metaphor in James 1:23-25.

[98] Genesis 1:26

[99] Genesis 1:28

[100] Mark 2:7

her husband murdered.[101] After repenting of this misdeed, he cried out to God "Against You, You only, I have sinned and done what is evil in Your sight."[102] David was fully aware that, while many others were hurt, ultimately his sin was directly an affront against God.

The Law of God demonstrates for us some practical working out of what it means to be an image bearer of God within creation. When Our Lord is asked what the Greatest Commandment is, He responds "'You shall love the Lord your God with all your heart, and with all your soul, and with all your mind.' ...The second is like it, 'You shall love your neighbor as yourself.'"[103] In other words, put God first in everything and love Him and those that bear His image. This gives us a standard to live by and helps us lead lives in an honoring way as God's ambassadors.

Here's the bad news: "All have sinned and fall short of the glory of God."[104] "No one is good except God alone."[105] "If we say that we have no sin, we are deceiving ourselves and the truth is not in us."[106] "All of us like sheep have gone astray, each of us has turned to his own way."[107] No one has met God's perfect standard of righteousness except God Himself in the person of Jesus Christ.

Let's let the Law do its job as a tutor and take a look at just the Ten Commandments. Have you ever told a lie?[108] God's Word is clear that for all liars, "their part will be in the lake that burns with fire."[109] Have you ever stolen something?[110] Remember that downloading

---

[101] 2 Samuel 11
[102] Psalm 51:4, NASB
[103] Matthew 22:37-39, NASB
[104] Romans 3:23, NASB
[105] Mark 10:18, NASB
[106] 1 John 1:8, NASB
[107] Isaiah 53:6, NASB
[108] This is the 9th Commandment, Exodus 20:16.
[109] Revelation 21:8, NASB
[110] This is the 8th Commandment, Exodus 20:15.

illegal music or calling sick into work when you're not is theft. Have you ever looked at someone other than your spouse with lust? God considers that adultery.[111] Have you put God first in your life at all times?[112] Have you made up a God in your own mind that you prefer to the True God?[113] Have you ever taken the Lord's name in vain?[114] God's Word states clearly that "the LORD will not leave him unpunished who takes His name in vain."[115] Have you kept the Sabbath?[116] Have you perfectly honored your parents?[117] Have you ever been angry with someone to the point of hatred? Our Lord defines this type of hateful anger as murder.[118] Lastly, have you ever jealously yearned for the money or possessions of another?[119]

Answering yes to any of these questions means that you are guilty of sin.

What does the mirror of the Law reflect in you? Have you borne the image of God well? If you feel like a failure, remember that you did fail. Keep in mind, "All have sinned and fall short of the glory of God."[120] The Law makes it crystal clear that I am not a good person, and neither are you. This is exactly why the Law leads us to an understanding of our need for the Gospel of Jesus Christ.[121]

---

[111] In Matthew 5:27-28, Our Lord expounds on the 7th Commandment
[112] This is the 1st Commandment, Exodus 20:3.
[113] This is the 2nd Commandment, Exodus 20:4-6.
[114] This is the 3rd Commandment, Exodus 20:7.
[115] Exodus 20:7, NASB
[116] This is the 4th Commandment, Exodus 20:8-9.
[117] This is the 5th Commandment, Exodus 20:12
[118] In Matthew 5:21-22, Our Lord expounds on the 6th Commandment.
[119] This is the 10th Commandment, Exodus 20:17.
[120] Romans 3:23, NASB
[121] This is Paul's point in Galatians 3:24.

God is Good

It can be tempting at this point to begin to compare ourselves to other people. In fact, I don't think I've ever gone through the Gospel with someone that they didn't at some point begin to justify their actions. For example, they'll say things like, "Sure, I've lied, but everyone lies every now and then." Or, sometimes, they'll pose a hypothetical scenario, "What if not lying would…"

This is why it's important to remember that we are not judged against the actions of other people. Our actions are compared to God's perfect standard. As far as all the hypotheticals, remember that these Commandments come from the very Creator of the Universe. He's the one that is Omniscient and beyond time. He's the one that tells us to follow His Laws. Therefore, in any given scenario, it's best to trust in Him rather than in our own limited assessment of the situation.[122]

Because of our own temptation to compare ourselves to other people, it is easy to develop this idea that "my sins" are not "that bad." However, in that thinking, we miss the biggest problem… God is good. As we discussed in the chapter on natural revelation, God is omnibenevolent- the very standard of what it means to be good. Because He is infinitely good, He hates all evil- including people who have done evil things.[123] Any evil action is so contrary to His nature that His perfect justice demands a proper punishment.

To illustrate this, I want you to imagine a serial killer. Let's say that this person has killed dozens of children. How do you feel about this person? Should this person be punished? Because most of us feel a great sense of protection towards children, we cannot even imagine what kind of evil person could do such a thing. The idea of harming

---

[122] Proverbs 3:5-6
[123] Psalm 5:5, Psalm 11:5, Proverbs 6:18, Proverbs 15, etc.

51

children is so far from most of our minds that we are able to rightly see it for the pure evil that it is. Our own sense of justice demands that this person be punished.

God is so good that every wrong action is like this to Him. Lying, cheating, stealing, lusting- these things are so contrary to His nature that He cannot let them go unpunished.

Think of a courtroom, and imagine a guilty person standing before the judge. If the judge knows that the person is guilty, could a good judge let the person go unpunished? Would a good judge allow a guilty person to go free because the judge liked the guilty person? No! This would be a wicked and biased judge. If the judge is aware that a person has committed a crime, then punishment must be carried out-regardless of how the judge feels towards the guilty person.

So, what is the penalty for sin? "The wages of sin is death..."[124] Death, properly understood in the Bible, means separation.[125] This is the punishment. For unregenerated persons, the Bible states that they "will pay the penalty of eternal destruction, away from the presence of the Lord and from the glory of His power."[126] This is called the second death.[127] In other words, at the final judgment, those that are unregenerated will be completely cut off from God and His glory.

You may remember from "The Grand Narrative" that glorifying God is our ultimate happiness. Given that, then what is it like to be completely cut off from the ultimate source of goodness? Our Lord

---

[124] Romans 6:23a, NASB

[125] Adam experienced death as God warned in Genesis 2:17 when he was cut off from a direct relationship with God that was available in the Garden. Physical death in Scripture is the separation of the soul from the body. Spiritual death is the separation of the soul from God.

[126] 2 Thessalonians 1:9, NASB

[127] Revelation 21:8

refers to this place of judgment as a "furnace of fire" and says that "in that place there will be weeping and gnashing of teeth."[128] Our Lord is also clear that this fire never goes out.[129]

Humans are eternal beings. Once conceived, we never cease to exist.[130] Being permanently separated from God is an eternal active torment that never ends, with absolutely no hope. It is pure terror, pain and destruction… forever.[131]

Who suffers this terrible death? God's Word is clear, "The person who sins will die."[132] Remember, God is good and He is a good judge. He cannot simply let evil deeds go unpunished because He likes someone. And, because every single sin is an act of rebellion against God and an attempted marring of His image, every sin has eternal and infinite consequences.

You and I fully deserve this eternal torment, and good works will not help us. Using the earthly judge metaphor again, imagine a guilty criminal standing before a good judge. The judge knows that the criminal is guilty of serious crimes. Now, imagine that this guilty criminal says to the judge "Yeah, ok, I've done that crime and I'm sorry about that, but look at all this other good stuff I did."[133] We inherently know that those good works are irrelevant. Wrong deeds were done, and any good judge would demand atonement.

Some may argue that we are taking the idea of an earthly justice system and imposing it on God. However, this view is exactly

---

[128] Matthew 13:42

[129] Mark 9:43

[130] In Matthew 25:46, humanity is split into two categories. The righteous go on to eternal life; the others will go on to eternal punishment.

[131] Revelation 21:8, Matthew 25:26, 2 Thessalonians 1:9, Matthew 13:50, Mark 9:43, Jude 1:7, 2 Peter 2:4, Matthew 10:28, etc.

[132] Ezekiel 18:20a, NASB

[133] This analogy is borrowed from Ray Comfort, president of Living Waters Ministry.

backwards. It is God's moral justice that forms the basis of our own legal system.[134] We rightly borrowed from Him, not the other way around.

Every sin must be paid for with an infinite price. Every single lie, act of theft, act of lust, anger, hatred, selfishness, lack of Godliness, every time we put ourselves first; all sins must be made right. Simply doing good deeds moving forward won't cover the wrong that has been done.

You may now be asking the question, "Well, who then can be saved?" Our Lord answered this question already, "With people this is impossible, but with God all things are possible."[135]

The Good News

The Law leaves us in a hopeless scenario and in desperate need of a Savior. The Good News is that He has come.

"He was pierced through for our transgressions, He was crushed for our iniquities; the chastening for our well-being fell upon Him, and by His scourging we are healed. All of us like sheep have gone astray, each of us has turned to his own way; but the Lord has caused the iniquity of us all to fall on Him."[136]

"God, being rich in mercy, because of His great love with which He loved us, even when we were dead in our transgressions, made us alive together with Christ."[137]

---

[134] Romans 13 makes this argument in Scripture wherein it argues that governments are largely created as a moral good to restrain/restrict evil.

[135] Matthew 19:26, NASB

[136] Isaiah 53:5-6, NASB

[137] Ephesians 2:4-5, NASB

"When you were dead in your transgressions and the uncircumcision of your flesh, He made you alive together with Him, having forgiven us all our transgressions, having canceled out the certificate of debt consisting of decrees against us, which was hostile to us; and He has taken it out of the way, having nailed it to the cross."[138]

For those alive in Christ, the debt for every single lie has been forgiven, every lust, every evil deed, every evil thought, every failure, every rebellion, every single act of disobedience; all of it is completely wiped clean.

How is this possible? We're told "He made Him who knew no sin to be sin on our behalf, so that we might become the righteousness of God in Him."[139] This is called imputation. Imputation is an accounting term which simply means the ascribing of value.[140] Value of the debt of our sins was ascribed to Our Lord, and the value of His earned righteousness was ascribed to us.

Imagine a guilty criminal is standing before a judge. The judge knows the criminal is guilty, but the judge has compassion on him/her. As we discussed, the judge cannot simply do away with the person's crimes because that would be wrong. Justice requires that the judge give the criminal the full penalty. So, the judge does exactly that. The judge gives the criminal the full sentence and charges him/her the full fine. In this way, justice is completely satisfied. Then the judge does something amazing. The judge takes off his/her robe, steps down from the bench and walks over amongst the criminals. The judge then pulls out his/her checkbook and pays for the fine in full on behalf of the criminal whom he had compassion on. In doing

---

[138] Colossians 2:13-14, NASB
[139] 2 Corinthians 5:21, NASB
[140] Bible Study Tools.
https://www.biblestudytools.com/dictionary/imputation/

this, the judge has done his job in satisfying the law and yet has also shown tremendous love for this guilty criminal. This is what God has done for us.[141]

As discussed in "The Grand Narrative", only God is capable of living up to the perfect standard of being an image bearer of God. Therefore, it took the life and work of Jesus Christ (both fully God and fully man) to live a perfect and sinless life. He earned the righteousness we had lost. He then gave up that righteousness by taking upon Himself the sins of the Church. Our sins were placed upon Him so that His righteousness could be placed upon us.[142] At His death, the sins of the Church were paid for in full. This is why Our Lord said "It is finished!"[143] as He died on the Cross.

"Therefore there is now no condemnation for those who are in Christ Jesus."[144] Not only is there no condemnation for those in Christ; but, even more amazingly, we are redeemed so that we may be regenerated (born-again). This means that we are made a totally new creation; one that desires to please and serve God. Putting 2 Corinthians 5:21 in context makes this point clear:
> ...if anyone is in Christ, he is a new creature; the old things passed away; behold, new things have come. Now all these things are from God, who reconciled us to Himself through Christ and gave us the ministry of reconciliation, namely, that God was in Christ reconciling the world to Himself, not counting their trespasses against them, and He has committed to us the word of reconciliation. Therefore, we are ambassadors for Christ, as though God were making an appeal through us; we beg you on behalf of Christ, be reconciled to God. He made Him who knew no

---

[141] This analogy is from Todd Friel of Wretched Radio/TV.
[142] Restatement of 2 Corinthians 5:21
[143] John 19:30, NASB
[144] Romans 8:1, NASB

sin to be sin on our behalf, so that we might become the righteousness of God in Him.[145]

We, through Christ, are saved not only from an eternity in Hell, but we are also saved from a life of sin. We are given the ability to resist sin in a way that we did not have prior to being born-again.

We are given a new love, a new heart. We begin to delight in that which pleases the Lord, and we begin to hate that which displeases Him. We are fully restored to a right relationship with God; even in this life.[146]

While many religions claim exclusivity on modes of achieving some eternal version of Heaven, only the Christian can say that he/she is going to Heaven and not be self-righteous.[147] Our hope is not in ourselves or in our works. We do not seek to reach a relationship with God through bribery or any other external means. The Christian's hope is built on nothing less than Jesus Christ and His righteousness.

A Christian is not inherently better than a non-believer. We are not saved because we're smarter or more obedient; we are saved because we are able to be declared righteous because of the work of Christ. This process of being made righteous is called being justified- which literally means to be declared righteous or pure.[148] We are justified by grace alone through faith alone in Christ alone as revealed in Scripture alone to the glory of God alone.[149]

---

[145] 2 Corinthians 5:17-21, NASB

[146] 1 Peter 5:10, 1 John 5:4, Matthew 6:33, etc.

[147] This is a loose quotation of a statement made by Paul Washer in the short-firm *American Gospel: Christ Alone.*
https://www.youtube.com/watch?v=ocHm18wUAGU

[148] Baker's Evangelical Dictionary of Biblical Theology.
https://www.biblestudytools.com/dictionary/justification/

[149] These are the Five Solae: Grace Alone, Faith Alone, Christ Alone, Scripture Alone and Glory to God Alone.

In other words, we are justified as a free gift (grace alone) and not because of anything that we did.[150] The gift that is given to us is the gift of a saving faith in Jesus Christ.[151] This gift is explained and spread through the Word of God alone.[152] In this way, all the glory for our salvation is to God alone. We deserve none of it.[153]

This is the glorious Gospel, the Good News. You and I were dead in our trespasses, with no hope. We had freely chosen to rebel against God, and so doing we deserved Hell. Our sins needed to be paid for, every one of them. Because of His love, the Father sent the Son, Jesus. Our Lord Jesus lived a perfect life earning a righteousness that He gave up on the Cross. The sins of the Church, the saved, were put upon Jesus and the debt owed was paid in full at His death. On the third day, He rose from the dead as assurance that death had indeed been defeated.

If you have not done so already, it is my earnest prayer that you recognize your own depravity. Recognize your need for a savior, then put your faith and trust in Jesus Christ as that savior. Repent of your sins by turning away from your sins and follow Christ as Lord of your life. In this way, you will be made a new creation. Your new heart will be one that desires to serve and love God and you will develop a love for His Word and His people, the Church.

Faith and Works

The relationship between faith and works is an important one to understand. There are two extremes that one can fall into and both

---

[150] Ephesians 2:8-9

[151] *Ibid.* The "it" that is a gift in this verse is faith.

[152] Romans 10:17, 1 Corinthians 1:17-18

[153] Colossians 2:13-14, John 3:16, Ephesians 2:1-7

are a departure from the Gospel of God. One extreme is called antinomianism or "easy-believism". This is the idea that once a person is saved, he/she can sin freely because of the work of the Cross. The other extreme is any requiring of works to be done apart from the Gospel of Christ. This is sometimes called a "faith and" heresy because it requires something more than a saving faith for justification. A "faith and" heresy can be easily identified because it's any teaching that says that something external to the atoning work of Christ is required for justification.

In Acts 15, the Apostles and the early Church had to deal with the issue of "faith and" head on. There were some Jewish converts in the early Church that were telling the Gentile converts that God will only accept them by His grace through faith AND the keeping of some of the ceremonial laws.[154] Paul recognized this as wrong immediately and headed to Jerusalem. There, "the apostles and the elders came together to look into this matter."[155] This gathering of the early Church is called the Jerusalem Counsel. At this counsel, Peter pronounced the following:

> Brethren, you know that in the early days God made a choice among you, that by my mouth the Gentiles would hear the word of the gospel and believe. And God, who knows the heart, testified to them giving them the Holy Spirit, just as He also did to us; and He made no distinction between us and them, cleansing their hearts by faith. Now therefore why do you put God to the test by placing upon the neck of the disciples a yoke which neither our fathers nor we have been able to bear? But we believe that we are saved through the grace of the Lord Jesus, in the same way as they also are.[156]

Notice the flow of the argument. Upon hearing the Gospel, they were given a new heart and a Holy Spirit. Peter then points out that

---

[154] Acts 15:1
[155] Acts 15:6, NASB
[156] Acts 15:7-11, NASB

all those which have the Holy Spirit are one, regardless of whatever they were before. He says that their hearts were cleansed by faith and that it's wrong to place additional burdens on them. Finally, he concludes by reminding them this faith is an act of grace and therefore nothing to be prideful about. It is a gift and one cannot earn a gift.

One may be tempted at this point to think that a Christian's actions are no longer of importance. This is untrue. Scripture is clear that "faith, if it has no works, is dead, being by itself."[157] The Apostle Paul predicts this reaction as he describes the Gospel in the Epistle to the Romans. In reaction to it, he writes:

What shall we say then? Are we to continue in sin so that grace may increase? May it never be! How shall we who died to sin still live in it? Or do you not know that all of us who have been baptized into Christ Jesus have been baptized into His death? Therefore we have been buried with Him through baptism into death, so that as Christ was raised from the dead through the glory of the Father, so we too might walk in newness of life. For if we have become united with Him in the likeness of His death, certainly we shall also be in the likeness of His resurrection, knowing this, that our old self was crucified with Him, in order that our body of sin might be done away with, so that we would no longer be slaves to sin; for he who has died is freed from sin.[158]

As we are born-again, our old selves die. We are made new, with a new heart that hates sin and loves the Lord. Previously we were a slave to sin, but having been freed from sin we are made slaves of Our Lord Jesus Christ.[159] We "have been bought with a price: therefore glorify God in your body."[160]

---

[157] James 2:17, NASB
[158] Romans 6:1-7, NASB
[159] Philippians 1:1, Romans 6, etc.
[160] 1 Corinthians 6:20, NASB

The Gospel is not that we are saved from damnation so that we can sin freely without fear of repercussion. Instead, the Gospel is that we are saved from the bondage of sin. Instead of being dead to, or separated from, God, we are made dead to sin and the worldly things of the fallen flesh. A saving faith produces works and not the other way around.

To put it simply, most worldviews/religions are about a series of things one most "do" to obtain some higher end. Christianity is about what has been done for you, and because of what was done, you will "do" certain things. These things that we do because of our saving faith are often referred to as fruit. If you want to test whether you or another person has a saving faith, then you can do so by looking for the presence of this spiritual fruit.[161]

"By this we know that we love the children of God, when we love God and observe His commandments. For this is the love of God, that we keep His commandments; and His commandments are not burdensome."[162] It is a joy to one who has been born-again to keep the commandments of God. This does not mean that we stop sinning perfectly once we're made new;[163] however, there is a shift in our heart. Whereas once it would have been heavily burdensome to try and keep the commandments of God, once we are made a new creation it is heavily burdensome not to keep the commandments. Rather than our passion being for the lusts of the flesh, our passion becomes will of God. "These things I have written to you who believe in the name of the Son of God, so that you may know that you have eternal life."[164] If we love God more than sin, then that love will produce good works.

---

[161] Matthew 7:16
[162] 1 John 5:2-3, NASB
[163] 1 John 1:8
[164] 1 John 5:13, NASB

If a person's life bears no fruit, then there is no reason to believe there is a saving faith.[165] If there is no faith, then there is no regeneration (rebirth).[166] If there is no regeneration (rebirth), then there is no salvation.[167] This is the relationship between faith and works.

Practicum

All of redemptive history would be a tragedy if it were not for the Gospel, and so too is each person's life a tragedy if it is not changed by the Gospel. If it were not for the fact that Jesus paid the penalty for our sins, then we would be eternally under the active wrath of God.

There is no repentant person in Hell. The torment is active and eternal because the rebellion is active and eternal. If it were not for the Good News of Jesus Christ, then the Grand Narrative would end at the Fall. Mankind would have failed, and the story would be of an infinitely good God and a tragically ruined Creation.

However, Jesus Christ did come, and those in Christ have been washed in the blood of the lamb and made spotless and pure. This is the answer to the death and futility of life around us.

Imagine that you're going to bed one night and you look out the window to see that your neighbor's house is on fire. Even worse, you see that they're home. You see that the fire is at the other end of the home, and they seem blissfully unaware of the rapidly spreading fire, Would you go on to bed? Would you thank the Lord that your house is ok and then head off to sleep?

---

[165] James 2:14-26
[166] 1 John 5:1
[167] John 3:3

Surely not! You would fling the door open and run over to their home. You'd pound on the door, and if they didn't answer, then you'd pound on the window. You would do whatever it took to alert and warn them.

If you're willing to do that out of concern for the sake of their earthly safety, then how much more so ought you to be willing to do that for the sake of their eternal life?

In Matthew 7, Our Lord Jesus exhorts us to "Enter through the narrow gate; for the gate is wide and the way is broad that leads to destruction, and there are many who enter through it. For the gate is small and the way is narrow that leads to life, and there are few who find it."[168] It is important to note that neither of these gates are marked "Hell." Both gates carry a promise of heaven, but only one of them leads there.

There are only two true religions in the world.

One religion tells you that you must do something to earn a particular desirable state (either heaven, happiness or some variation thereof). The false theistic religions of the world fall into this category. In fact, even atheism and agnosticism fall into this category as they carry with them other moral ideologies such as hedonism, which states that the way to happiness is through serving one's own desires.

The other religion is Christianity, the Grand Narrative, which states that we exist for the glory of God and that all of Creation is from Him, through Him, in Him and for Him. No person is perfectly good, and no perfectly good God could let a single sin go unpaid for. Thus, He is our only hope. Jesus Christ alone is the only hope of humanity.[169]

---

[168] Matthew 7:13-14, NASB
[169] John 14:6

If you know this to be true, and you care about other people even a little bit, then it is not possible for you to go through your day-to-day life without regularly sharing the Gospel with others. A doctor that has a cure and doesn't tell the diseased is guilty of malpractice. A person that goes on to sleep while knowing that his neighbor is in trouble is evil and selfish. A person that puts their own comfort before the eternal needs of those around him or her is failing miserably at both of the great commandments.[170]

Obey your Lord and go into all the world. Preach the Gospel and make disciples![171]

---

[170] Matthew 22:36-40; A person cannot love God in such a way and treat others in such a way and not regularly share their faith.

[171] Matthew 28:16-20

-6-
THE TRINITY

Perhaps the most misunderstood and yet essential doctrine of the Christian faith is that of the Trinity. Very few evangelicals seem to be able to articulate exactly what the Trinity is or why we believe in it.

Perhaps for this very reason, the Trinity is often where the cultic apologists attack. Muslim apologists, Mormons and Jehovah's Witnesses are almost definitely going to challenge the doctrine of the Trinity within the first meeting. This is because it's a fruitful place for them to attack since the average Christian is very weak on this topic.

Even within our own Sunday Schools and private Christian Schools, our well-intentioned teachers are constantly teaching accidental heresy.

Let's start by saying that it is not true that the doctrine of the Trinity is something that no one can understand. While certainly there are many aspects of God and His inner workings that are not revealed to us and that we do not and cannot fully comprehend (i.e. the concept of eternity), that does not mean that we cannot communicate and understand the attributes clearly revealed in Scripture.

The Nicene Creed

The Nicene Creed will help guide this topic.[172] It's a common tactic of neo-Atheists and cultic apologists to say that the doctrine of the Trinity was "invented" in the Nicene Creed, but thats easily proven false.

For one thing, no council ever called by the early church was gathered in order to invent doctrine. These councils were always to combat heresies that gained popularity. The Council of Nicea was first convened to combat Arianism, which was the idea that Jesus was merely a part of creation. Then later, they met to combat Modalism. The reality is that these councils were convened to compare teachings to Scripture, and whatever was found to be in conflict with Scripture was condemned. These were not meetings where a bunch of faithful Christians and early church leaders came together in order to make up whatever they wanted to. They were gathered together in order to identify and condemn false teachings; using Scripture to identify what is and is not true.

Due to these early church councils, we get a good summary of what the Christian Church throughout history has believed about specific topics like the Trinity. We also have some helpful language to discuss these truths without committing accidental blasphemy. This is why creeds like this are helpful. They provide guardrails to keep us from error.

---

[172] Technically I'm using the Niceno-Constantinopolitan Creed

The Nicene Creed:[173]

I believe in One God,
the Father Almighty,
Maker of Heaven and Earth,
and of all things visible and invisible.

And in one Lord Jesus Christ,
the Son of God,
the Only-Begotten, begotten of the Father before all ages;
Light of Light;
True God of True God;
begotten, not made;
of one essence with the Father,
by Whom all things were made;
Who for us men and for our salvation
came down from Heaven,
and was incarnate of the Holy Spirit and the Virgin Mary,
and became man.
And He was crucified for us under Pontius Pilate,
and suffered, and was buried.
And the third day He arose again,
according to the Scriptures,
and ascended into Heaven,
and sits at the right hand of the Father;
and He shall come again with glory to judge the living and the dead;
Whose Kingdom shall have no end.

And in the Holy Spirit, the Lord, the Giver of Life,

---

[173] This version is from the Orthodox Christian Fellowship at MIT except that the author has added the filioque clause of "and the son" after "who proceeds from the Father" in order to correct what we view to be their error in translation/tradition. http://web.mit.edu/ocf/www/nicene_creed.html

Who proceeds from the Father and the Son;
Who with the Father and the Son together is worshipped and
glorified;
Who spoke by the prophets.

And in One, Holy, Catholic, and Apostolic Church.

I acknowledge one baptism for the remission of sins.
I look for the resurrection of the dead,
and the life of the world to come.

This creed gives us some clear guidelines in how we can describe
the Holy Trinity. It is much better to memorize a creed like this than it
is to consistently use a given metaphor.

Problem of Metaphors

While metaphors and analogies can be very helpful tools to help us
understand something, much of the damage that has been done to the
doctrine of the Trinity in our modern age is the frequency with which
we offer physical metaphors to describe the inner workings of the
Holy Trinity.

For example, you may have heard that the Trinity is like water
because water can be a solid, liquid and gas but it is still water.
Likewise, you may also have heard someone use the fact that one
person can be a father, a husband and a minister but he is still one
person. The problem with both of those is that they are technically a
heresy called Sabellianism or Modalism. A single molecule of water
can only exist in a single state, and a single person is still the same
person regardless of what role that person is occupying.

The God of the Bible is not one person playing various roles. This particular heresy keeps the fact that there is one God, but loses the clear teaching from Scripture that the three separate persons of the Trinity are indeed 3 separate persons.

To combat that, sometimes a person will use the metaphor of some type of oligarchy where three kings are co-regents and ruling a kingdom together. The problem with this metaphor of the Trinity is that it leads to a heresy known as Tritheism. It hyper-exemplifies the three persons of the Trinity but completely demolishes the fact that God is one being.

So ultimately, what metaphor can be used to describe the Trinity? Nothing. Simply put, there is nothing in our physical creation that we live in that accurately and exactly communicates the Triune nature of the Holy God. Using one almost certainly leads you to one heresy or the other.

Simply because there is no metaphor that does not mean that we can't understand the Trinity. This core doctrine is clearly described in Scripture and so it is absolutely a Truth we can understand.

The Trinitarian Absolutes

Perhaps the best way to understand the Trinity is to list out all the things that are clearly and absolutely revealed about this attribute of God from Scripture. Any compromise on these absolutes leads to a detriment of the Gospel and a contradiction to God's revealed Word about Himself.

Absolute 1: There is only one God.[174]
- As the Shema says, "Hear, O Israel! The Lord is our God, the Lord is one!"[175] The Trinity is not polytheism- we worship one God and one God alone. The Bible is very clear on this point in both New and Old Testament.

The Scripture is also clear that this one God we serve is made up of three separate persons.

Absolute 2: The father is God.[176]
- This is relatively uncontested unlike the other two members of the Holy Trinity.

Absolute 3: The Son is God.
- He is specifically referred to as God.[177]
- Jesus also is given many of the same titles as God.[178]
- Jesus received the honor due only to God.[179]
- Jesus has many of the attributes that are God's alone, for example, omnipresence.[180]
- Jesus is eternal. He was not created.[181]

---

[174] Deut. 4:35; 4:39; 32:39; 2 Sam. 22:32; Isa. 37:20: 43:10; 44:6-8; 45:5; 45:14; 45:21-22; 46:9; John 5:44; Rom. 3:30; 16:27; 1 Cor. 8:4-6; Gal. 3:20; Eph. 4:6; 1 Tim. 1:17; 1 Tim. 2:5; James 2:19; Jude 25

[175] Deuteronomy 6:4, NASB

[176] John 17:3; 1 Cor. 8:6; 2 Cor. 1:3; Eph. 1:3;1 Pet. 1:3

[177] Isa. 9:6; Isa. 10:21; John 1:1-5; Mark 12:27; Luke 20:38; John 8:54; Phil 2:13; Heb. 11:16; Mark 12:27; Luke 20:37-38; John 3:2; 13:3; Rom. 1:21; 1 Thess. 1:9; Heb. 9:14; 1 Pet. 4:10-11; John 1:18; John 20:28; Psa. 35:23; John 20:17; Acts 20:28; Rom. 9:5; Titus 2:13; 2 Thess. 2:8; 1 Tim. 6:14; 2 Tim. 1:10; 4:1, 4:8; Heb. 1:8; 2 Pet. 1:11; and 1 John 5:20

[178] Luke 2:11; John 4:42; 1 John 4:14; Titus 2:13, Titus 2:10; Isa. 43:11; 45:21-22; and 1 Tim. 4:10

[179] Matt. 28:17; Heb. 1:6; and Matt 4:10

[180] Matt. 18:20; 28:20; John 3:13; Eph. 1:23; 4:10; and Col. 3:11

[181] John 1:1; 8:58; 17:5; Col. 1:17; and Heb. 1:2

- The fact that Jesus is begotten is clear in Scripture and is even referenced in the Nicene Creed. However, it is critical to note that begotten does not mean created. All things were made through Jesus, and apart from Jesus, nothing was made. The idea of "begotten son" is a reference to His role within the eternal Godhead and not to the idea that He was ever not existent.

Absolute 4: The Holy Spirit is God.
- He is equated to God.[182]
- He is eternal,[183] omnipresent[184] and omniscient.[185]
- He was also involved in Creation.[186]

So far, we know that the Bible has made clear there is only one God, and we know that the Father, the Son and the Holy Spirit are God. How do we know that these three are indeed separate persons? Matthew 28:19 and the clear use of the definitive article "the" is one indication. The verse reads, "Go therefore and make disciples of all the nations, baptizing them in the name of the Father and the Son and the Holy Spirit."[187]

Absolute 5: Jesus is not the Father.[188]
- If Jesus and the Father were the same person, then the prayer in the Garden would make no sense. The whole prayer would be essentially a stage-play, making Jesus a hypocrite which is the Greek word for actor.

---

[182] Acts 5:3-4; 2 Cor. 3:17-18
[183] Heb. 9:14
[184] Psa. 139:7
[185] 1 Cor. 2:10-11
[186] Gen. 1:2; Psa. 104:30
[187] Matthew 28:19, NASB
[188] Rom. 1:7; 1 Cor. 1:3; 2 Cor. 1:2; Gal. 1:3; Eph. 1:2; 6:23; Phil. 1:2; 1 Thess. 1:1; 2 Thess. 1:1-2; 1 Tim. 1:1-2; 2 Tim. 1:2; Tit. 1:4; James 1:1; 2 Pet. 1:2; 2 John 3; John 3:16-17; Gal. 4:4; 1 John 4:10; John 3:35; 5:20; 14:31; 15:9; 17:23-26; cf. Matt. 3:17 par.; Matt. 17:5 par.; 2 Pet. 1:17; Matt. 11:27; Luke 10:22; John 7:29; 8:55; and 10:15

- It is the person of the Son, Jesus Christ our Lord and Savior that was made fully man, and sent by the Father.[189]
- Jesus has a specific and distinct role in redemptive history.

Absolute 6: Jesus is not the Holy Spirit.[190]
- "But when He, the Spirit of truth, comes, He will guide you into all the truth; for He will not speak on His own initiative, but whatever He hears, He will speak; and He will disclose to you what is to come. He will glorify Me, for He will take of Mine and will disclose it to you."- Jesus, John 16:13-14 (NASB). In this verse, Jesus makes it absolutely clear that the Spirit is a person, and that He is a person separate from Jesus.
- In Luke 3:22 and the parallel verses[191] in the other Gospels, it would be nonsensical that He should descend upon Himself.

Absolute 7: The Holy Spirit is not the Father.[192]
- "When the Helper comes, whom I will send to you from the Father, that is the Spirit of truth who proceeds from the Father, He will testify about Me,"- Jesus, John 15:26 (NASB). Obviously if the Spirit proceeds, which in the Greek is ἐκπορεύομαι (ekporeuomai) or to depart, from the Father, then He is not the Father since one cannot depart from Himself.

Absolute 8: There is one God made up of three distinct persons (the Father, the Son and the Holy Spirit).
- The Holy Spirit is a distinct person, fully God. Jesus, the Son, is a distinct person that became fully man in the

---

[189] John 3:16
[190] John 14:16; John 15:26; 16:7; John 16:13-14; Luke 3:22
[191] Mark 1:10, John 1:32 and Matthew 3:16
[192] John 14:16; 15:26; Rom. 8:26-27

incarnation and yet at all times is fully eternal and fully God. Finally, the Father is a distinct person and fully God.

When you put all of these things together, then you come to the same conclusion as those throughout Church history. There is one God and this God is one in essence and three in personhood.

Practicum

God is love.[193]

This should not be confused with the idea that God is merely loving; for there are many who are loving. However, the Truth that God is love means far more than that. He is, in Himself, that which we call love.

There is something about the relationship between a person and something outside of that person that is equated to an objective standard that we call love. Just like the concept of something as being "good" requires a universal, objective standard of good, so too does love require an objective standard.

It is the beautiful doctrine of the Trinity that helps us understand what is meant by the fact that God is love. He is love because within Himself is the absolute relationship of persons; the absolute, objective standard of love. The relationship which is characterized as a beautiful blend of submission, obedience, care, unity, service and yet perfect equality. This relationship is where we derive the concept that we call love.

---

[193] 1 John 4:8

Furthermore, this doctrine helps make sense of all of redemptive history. Given that all things exist to glorify God, each person of the Trinity must be glorified in specific ways. The Father is glorified in creation and election. The Son is glorified in obedience and sacrifice, and the Spirit is glorified in revelation and sanctification.

Absolutely all of redemptive history is about a Triune God that is seeking the absolute best possible purpose; which is to glorify Himself.

-7-

JESUS, THE CHRIST

From the very moment of the Fall, Adam and Eve were promised a coming savior that would crush their enemy and restore humanity to a right relationship with God.[194] The whole of the Old Testament is the story of a people awaiting the coming Savior. The New Testament begins with the Gospels; the Good News that He has come. And the remainder of the New Testament is instruction and promises to a people that have been redeemed by the Savior and await His coming again at the ultimate end of the age.

The Preeminent One

Let's unpack Colossians 1:15-20 (NASB) because it contains so much amazing Truth about Our Lord Jesus Christ:

---

[194] Genesis 3:15

He is the image of the invisible God, the firstborn of all creation. For by Him all things were created, both in the heavens and on earth, visible and invisible, whether thrones or dominions or rulers or authorities—all things have been created through Him and for Him. He is before all things, and in Him all things hold together. He is also head of the body, the church; and He is the beginning, the firstborn from the dead, so that He Himself will come to have first place in everything. For it was the Father's good pleasure for all the fullness to dwell in Him, and through Him to reconcile all things to Himself, having made peace through the blood of His cross; through Him, I say, whether things on earth or things in heaven.

First of all, we're told that He is the image of the invisible God. Jesus Himself says that "He who has seen Me has seen the Father."[195] John 1:18 says that Jesus, the Son, ἐξηγέομαι (exēgeomai) the Father. This is the Greek word that we get the English word exegete from. It means "to fully draw out." When a teacher exegetes a book, the teacher unpacks all that is contained within. In other words, the teacher shows the student the full meaning of the book. This is what Scripture teaches that the Son does- He exegetes the Father to us. He is the very image of the invisible God.

He is the firstborn of all creation. This does not mean that He was created Himself. Indeed, Scripture is very clear that He has always been in existence; fully eternal and beyond time.[196] Firstborn of all creation is a specific title that means He is the inheritor of all creation, which He is.[197]

This passage also tells us that He created all things, and that all things were created for Him. You exist for Christ, the flowers exist for

---

[195] John 14:9
[196] John 1:1; 8:58; 17:5; Col. 1:17; and Heb. 1:2
[197] Hebrews 1:2; John 3:35; and Psalm 2:7-8;

Christ, the fish in the sea exist for Christ. All of Creation is for, through and because of Him.

He is before all things and He is the sustainer of all of creation.

He is the head of the Church. He was the first to rise in a glorified body. And we know that all things are reconciled to the Father through Jesus Christ, Our Lord.

The Redeemer

Jesus alone is the hope of mankind for salvation. If you don't think that it's important to understand who Jesus actually is, just remember that Jesus told His disciples that "Unless you believe that I am He, you will die in your sins."[198] This is one reason why it is a Gospel issue for someone to deny who Our Lord actually is. The term "I am He" is a direct reference to His deity.[199] If Jesus is not fully God, then His atonement is not infinite, nor is it logical that any being other than God could be as good as God.

Remember, that because of God's goodness, no sin can go without repayment. He is so good that every single wrong action must be made right. This is a right and good action, but it is also a terrifying reality because "all have sinned and fallen short of the glory of God."[200]

Every other religion and way of thinking in the world is concerned with trying to be good enough to earn favor or reward. Christianity,

---

[198] John 8:24 (NASB)

[199] In Hebrew, the phrase "I am" (אֶהְיֶה , ehyeh) such as used in Exodus 3:14 is related to the personal covenant name of God- יהוה (YHWH- which is said in English as Yahweh or Jehovah).

[200] Romans 3:23 (NASB)

however, is unique in that it is entirely about Jesus Christ. Only Christianity addresses the logical problem that a good God cannot merely look the other way at sin. Only Christianity shows a loving and kind God that prepares a way of salvation for His people; while also remaining a consistent and fully just God that punishes all evil.

It turns out that the only person capable of being as good as God is God Himself, in the person of Jesus Christ.

Person and Work of Christ

To understand the work that Our Lord did for us, let's take a look at another passage. Philippians 2:6-8 (NASB) says:
...although He existed in the form of God, did not regard equality with God a thing to be grasped, but emptied Himself, taking the form of a bond-servant, and being made in the likeness of men. Being found in appearance as a man, He humbled Himself by becoming obedient to the point of death, even death on a cross.

The preexistent, fully God, second person of the Trinity humbled Himself even to the point of coming in the flesh as a human being. He was born of the Virgin Mary[201] into a very real, fully human body. In His human nature, He relied upon the ministry of the Holy Spirit[202] and upon the revealed Word of God.[203] He led a life of perfect obedience, without sin.[204] Therefore, He alone fulfilled the Law and earned the eternal reward. He had satisfied the Law fully.

---

[201] Matthew 1:18
[202] Isaiah 11:1-3; Luke 4:1
[203] John 7:15
[204] 1 Peter 2:22; 2 Corinthians 5:21

In His life He was a man of sorrows and acquainted with grief.[205] He had to endure the full hardships of life on earth.[206] Out of obedience to the Father and out of love for the Church, He gave up the reward that He earned. Instead, our sins were placed on Him and He bore the burden of those sins.[207] In His death on the cross, He was pierced for our transgressions.[208] In this way, the penalty for the sins of the Church, those in Christ, was paid for in full.[209]

On the third day, He rose from the dead; defeating death for all of those who are in Christ.[210] After some time with the Apostles and others, being seen by more than 500 people,[211] He ascended into heaven and is "at the right hand of God, having gone into heaven, after angels and authorities and powers had been subjected to Him."[212] He will come again in the same way at the end of this age.[213]

Practicum

Our Lord Jesus Christ is everything to us. For those of us in the Church (which is the body of Christ), God had compassion upon us despite our sins. Jesus Christ came down from His exalted position to be among the guilty, although He Himself is innocent, and He paid the fine that we could not pay. In this way, every single sin is paid for, every single wrong is made right and we can inherit the amazing freedom and the great reward even though we were guilty.

---

[205] Isaiah 53:3
[206] Hebrews 4:15
[207] 2 Corinthians 5:21
[208] Isaiah 53; Psalm 22
[209] 1 John 2:2
[210] 1 Corinthians 15:55-57
[211] 1 Corinthians 15:6
[212] 1 Peter 3:22
[213] Acts 1:9-11

Jesus is our ultimate prophet in that He not only communicated God's Word to us[214] but also in that He Himself is the Word of God made flesh.[215] We know more about God than could have ever been possible prior to the incarnation of Christ because of the life and works of Jesus Christ.[216] Also, just like the Old Testament prophets, He confirmed His Word with miracles.[217]

Jesus is our ultimate priest because, just like the Old Testament priests, He prays to God on the behalf of His people.[218] However, whereas the Old Testament priests offered sacrifices on behalf of the people; Jesus IS the sacrifice offered on behalf of His people.[219]

In addition to being our prophet and priest, Jesus Christ is our king. Just as the Old Testament foretold,[220] just as the wise men pronounced at His birth,[221] just as He Himself professed during His life,[222] and just as His disciples recognized before, during and after His ascension,[223] Jesus Christ is our King. We are to be good soldiers in His army.[224]

Whereas, before we were born again, we were like the first Adam; fallen and in rebellion to God. After being born again we are like the second Adam; who was the perfect human, fully God and fully man, which offered Himself for our sakes. Either we serve the second

---

[214] Matthew 21:11; Luke 7:16; John 4:19; Mark 6:4; Acts 3:17–23; 7:37–38, 51–53

[215] John 1:1; John 1:14

[216] Deuteronomy 18:15

[217] Matthew 8:1–17; 9:18–33; Mark 1:32–34; 2:1–12; Luke 17:11–19; 18:35–43; John 2:1–11; 6:1–24

[218] John 17:1-26

[219] Hebrews 4:14-16; Hebrews 10:19-23

[220] Micah 5:2; Isaiah 9:6; Exodus 15:18; Psalm 45:6; etc.

[221] Matthew 2:2

[222] Matthew 21:5; Matthew 27:11

[223] 1 Timothy 6:15; Philippians 2:9-11

[224] 2 Timothy 2:3

Adam, Jesus Christ, and recognize Him as our Savior and Lord, or we will die in our sins.[225]

---

[225] John 8:24

-8-
THE HOLY SPIRIT

The Gospel is truly a Trinitarian Gospel. The Father, in His goodness, sends the Son[226] and sets aside His Church.[227] The Son, Jesus Christ, offers Himself as the atoning sacrifice on our behalf. His righteousness is accredited to those in Christ and the sins of those in Christ were paid for upon the Cross.[228] It is the Holy Spirit that convicts the heart of the believer to reveal that Jesus is Lord.[229]

Our Advocate

After explaining to His disciples that it is actually a good thing that the Cross and ascension take place, Jesus says this of the Spirit in John 16:7-11 (NASB):

---

[226] John 3:16
[227] John 6:44
[228] 2 Corinthians 5:21
[229] 1 Corinthians 12:3

I will send [the Spirit, the Helper] to you. And He, when He comes, will convict the world concerning sin and righteousness and judgment; concerning sin, because they do not believe in Me; and concerning righteousness, because I go to the Father and you no longer see Me; and concerning judgment, because the ruler of this world has been judged.

This is an amazing Truth because it means that, as we share our faith with others, we have an advocate on the inside. God Himself in the Spirit will convict the heart of the sinner and reveal the Truth of Jesus Christ when the Gospel is shared rightly from the Word.[230]

The Word of God itself is the work of the Holy Spirit. The Apostle Peter reminds us in 1 Peter 1:21 that the Bible is not just a work of men, but rather that "men moved by the Holy Spirit spoke from God."[231] This gives the Bible full and ultimate authority as it is the special revelation of God Himself through the Third Person of the Trinity.[232]

It is by the Holy Spirit that you are baptized into the body of Jesus Christ.[233] All of those in Christ are indwelt with the Holy Spirit, and it is this gift of the Holy Spirit that enables us to really grow in godliness.[234] The Spirit "will guide you into all the truth."[235] He is our "helper" and our connection to Jesus Christ in throughout our life.[236] He is also the source of specific gifts which are given to each member of the body of Christ to equip that particular member for the specific role that he or she is to play in redemptive history.[237]

---

[230] Romans 10:17; John 15:26
[231] 1 Peter 1:21 (NASB)
[232] 2 Timothy 3:16-17
[233] 1 Corinthians 12:13
[234] Romans 8:9
[235] John 16:13
[236] John 14:16
[237] 1 Corinthians 12

The Spirit's Temple

Having the very Spirit of God inside you is an amazing gift. It is also an amazing responsibility. The inner most part of the temple was called the "Holy of Holies" because it was in this place that the Holy Spirit was said to dwell. When a priest would enter into the Holy of Holies, he would be extremely careful because he knew that if he made an error, then he would be killed instantly.[238] Why? Well, Moses tells us after one such incident. Aaron's sons offer strange fire to the Lord... and they are killed for doing so. Aaron goes to Moses to complain and Moses reminds Aaron that the Lord had said "By those who come near Me, I will be treated as holy; and before all the people I will be honored."[239]

If any of us were chosen to go into the Holy of Holies, we would rightly do so with a certain amount of concern and sober mindedness. We would be on high alert, making sure that we did everything perfectly. Well, for us in Christ after the day of Pentecost, when the Holy Spirit descended on the Church, WE ARE the dwelling place of the Holy Spirit. This Truth should guide our lives accordingly.

As the Apostle Paul put it when he wrote the Church in Corinth, "do you not know that your body is a temple of the Holy Spirit who is in you, whom you have from God, and that you are not your own? For you have been bought with a price: therefore glorify God in your body."[240]

---

[238] Leviticus 10:1-2
[239] Leviticus 10:3 (NASB)
[240] 1 Corinthians 6:19-20 (NASB)

Our Helper, Our Seal

Thankfully, it is none other than the Holy Spirit Himself that aides us in glorifying God. Once you have been born again and the Holy Spirit takes up residence in you, you will bear the fruit of the Spirit. Your flesh is still there, and you will constantly battle between your sinful flesh and the Spirit of God,[241] but the Spirit will make Himself known in you through the fruit.

"...The fruit of the Spirit is love, joy, peace, patience, kindness, goodness, faithfulness, gentleness, self-control; against such things there is no law."[242] Paul goes on in this passage to remind us that "those who belong to Christ Jesus have crucified the flesh with its passions and desires. If we live by the Spirit, let us also walk by the Spirit."[243]

In other words, if you are in Christ, then your flesh is crucified/dead. Therefore, rather than doing what your sinful flesh wants to do, you are to live in accord and harmony with the Holy Spirit who is in you.

It is in this very way that you may have assurance of your salvation. The Holy Spirit and the fruit that He produces in your life is your guarantee.[244] It is an ever increasing death of your sinful flesh and an increase in Christlikeness.

"...After listening to the message of truth, the gospel of your salvation—having also believed, you were sealed in [Jesus] with the Holy Spirit of promise, who is given as a pledge of our inheritance,

---

[241] Galatians 5:17
[242] Galatians 5:22-23
[243] Galatians 5:24-25
[244] 2 Corinthians 1:22; 1 John 5

with a view to the redemption of God's own possession, to the praise of His glory."[245]

Practicum

You were called by the Father, who in His love and mercy sent His Son Jesus Christ. Jesus Christ, in His perfect obedience earned a righteousness that we could not earn, and being fully human and fully God, He offered Himself as the sacrifice on our behalf so that we may be restored to a right relationship. Once restored, we are given the seal of that salvation. He is the Holy Spirit, who lives in us and helps us glorify God throughout our lives.

All of Creation is the story of one perfect being, made up of 3 persons, glorifying each person throughout redemptive history.

While you will always struggle with sin throughout your life in this age, your flesh should consistently lose that battle and the Spirit in you should be more and more evident throughout your days. If you do not submit yourself to the Spirit, if you are not showing the fruit of the Holy Spirit or showing evidence that He lives in you, then you should have absolutely no confidence in your salvation.

---

[245] Ephesians 1:13-14 (NASB)

-9-
THE CHURCH

For centuries, the Jewish people gathered together at the Temple to worship near the dwelling place of the Holy Spirit. Then one glorious day, the day of Pentecost, the Holy Spirit descended upon the disciples of Christ. Suddenly the people became the Temple since the Holy Spirit now dwells inside them. This event marks the beginning of the age in which we live- the Church Age.

Body of Christ

A man named Saul of Tarsus ravaged the early Church, raiding houses and throwing men and women in jail merely for following Jesus.[246] He was present and complicit in the killing of the first

---

[246] Acts 8:3

Christian martyr.[247] The exploits of Saul and his persecution of the Christians spread across the region.[248] Jesus appeared before this man who tormented the Church, and Our Lord asked this man "Saul, Saul, why do you persecute me?"[249]

Saul of Tarsus ended up being converted by Jesus in this encounter and went on to be the Apostle Paul, writer of the majority of the New Testament. Notice that Jesus asked why Saul was persecuting *ME*. This lets us in on an amazing Truth. Saul was persecuting believers; he was persecuting the Church, and yet Jesus asks him about persecuting *ME*.

This reveals the reality that the Church is the body of Christ. The Apostle Paul, the same one that was Saul of Tarsus, tells us exactly this in 1 Corinthians 12:12-27:

For even as the body is one and yet has many members, and all the members of the body, though they are many, are one body, so also is Christ. For by one Spirit we were all baptized into one body, whether Jews or Greeks, whether slaves or free, and we were all made to drink of one Spirit. For the body is not one member, but many... you are Christ's body, and individually members of it.

In this same chapter, Paul uses the metaphor of a physical body to relate the concept that we all have different roles in the body of Christ. An ear is great at hearing, but it makes a terrible foot. If you are a foot, be the absolute greatest foot you can be for the glory of God. If you are an ear, be the greatest possible ear. Be happy with your gifts and use them to the glory of God. The reason for this is because the Church has many needs, and it needs your specific gifts.[250]

---

[247] Acts 7:58-8:1
[248] Acts 9:13-14
[249] Acts 9:4
[250] 1 Corinthians 12 paraphrased

Holy Assembly

The word "church" in Greek is Εκκλησία (ecclesia) and it means "assembly" or "called out ones."[251] It is important to remember that the Church is not a geographic location or a place that you can go to. In other words, the commonly heard phrase "let's go to Church" is technically nonsensical because Church is not a place. Likewise, the Church is not an earthly institution. It is the very living body of Christ and Jesus Christ Himself is the head of the Church.[252]

As a born-again believer, you are a part of the universal and holy assembly now known as the Church. The Church is a holy gathering of persons to worship God in total unison with one another.[253] When you have the Holy Spirit in your heart, you are a part of this royal priesthood.[254] Because you have Jesus Christ as your high priest[255] and because you have the Holy Spirit working in you and upon you,[256] you can directly approach the throne of God in worship and in prayer. This is an amazing privilege; a more direct relationship with God than mankind has enjoyed since the Garden.

At the end of this age, we will see God face-to-face and have an even greater and more direct and immediate relationship than what we get a sense of in this life.[257]

---

[251] Strong's Concordance #1577
[252] Ephesians 1:22-23
[253] Psalm 22:25; Psalm 149:1
[254] 1 Peter 2:5
[255] Hebrews 4:14-16
[256] Romans 8:26-27
[257] Revelation 21

The Universal Church

The Church is a unified whole. There is only one actual Church. Those born again and placed in Christ are one. While there may be many denominations which disagree on a multitude of secondary issues, the reality is that there is no saved person outside of the body of Christ and He only has one body, one bride. As Paul wrote to the Ephesians, "There is one body and one Spirit, just as also you were called in one hope of your calling; one Lord, one faith, one baptism, one God and Father of all who is over all and through all and in all."[258]

The amazing reality is that while each person has his or her role within the Church, we are all united as one and equal. Regardless of gender, race, age, nationality, socio-economic status, we are all one in Christ Jesus.[259]

In like manner, we are to strive together in unity and seek fellowship with one another through our savior Jesus Christ. We are to seek to be like-minded, striving to be in-step with the same mind; the mind of Christ.[260] As born-again believers, we are to live amongst each other in peace with a unified love toward one another.[261]

Peter, with the Holy Spirit, gives us the perfect guidelines for how we are to interact with one another:
To sum up, all of you be harmonious, sympathetic, brotherly, kindhearted, and humble in spirit; not returning evil for evil or insult for insult, but giving a blessing instead; for you were called for the very purpose that you might inherit a blessing.[262]

---

[258] Ephesians 4:4-6 (NASB)
[259] Ephesians 2:14; Romans 12:16; Galatians 3:26-28
[260] 1 Corinthians 1:10
[261] 2 Corinthians 13:11
[262] 1 Peter 3:8-9 (NASB)

Remember, you are a part of the Lord's Army. No army can be effective on the battlefield when there is in-fighting and disharmony among the troops.

Life Together

Do not forget that, as a part of the body of Christ, you are needed to be active in the body. "Let us hold fast the confession of our hope without wavering, for He who promised is faithful; and let us consider how to stimulate one another to love and good deeds, not forsaking our own assembling together, as is the habit of some, but encouraging one another; and all the more as you see the day drawing near."[263]

The Church draws its authority from the Word of God; which is the only infallible source of knowledge.[264] Scripture draws its authority from God, but the Church draws its authority from the Word of God and is therefore to submit to the Word of God on all matters.[265]

In summary, the Church is the unified body of Christ made up of all born-again believers. The Church should strive towards harmony towards one another with a humble heart and a desire to do the will of God in accordance with His Revealed Word in the Bible. Believers are to be an active member of a regular assembly of the Church in order to receive encouragement as well as to give encouragement to others.

---

[263] Hebrews 10:23-25 (NASB)
[264] 2 Timothy 3:16-17
[265] Acts 17:11; the Bereans are commended for recognizing that the Scripture's authority is derived from within Scripture

Practicum

You are a soldier in battle.[266] You are to live as such. You have enemies that seek to destroy you. Those around you have enemies and are actively under attack. There are many dying, both physically and spiritually.

You are different from the World, you are separated from the World, called out from the World. As such, you scrape and battle constantly. Your Commander, your Lord Jesus Christ, has given you an amazing gift beginning on the day of Pentecost; the Church of Christ which is unified in the Holy Spirit.

The assembly of the Church, the assembly of believers in Christ to worship God and grow in Christlikeness together is an amazing opportunity to rest from battle.

There are many brothers and sisters who often confuse reading the Bible or going to a Church assembly as an act of service to God. That's simply not the case. While it is definitely an act of obedience, because after all you have been told to do both of those things, Scripture and the Church are gifts to you.

Going to Church is like a soldier returning to a home base while being deployed in a foreign land. The Church assembly is where you go to rest and recharge. It is where you go to be resupplied, refreshed and better equipped for when you return to the battle.

If you do not regularly attend a local Church assembly, then you are not only going against Scripture[267], but you are also missing out on the opportunity to experience one of God's greatest gifts to believers in this age.

---

[266] Ephesians 6
[267] Hebrews 10:25

-10-
THE BELIEVER

As a born-again Christian and a member of the Lord's Army, how then are you to conduct yourself throughout your life?

Let's begin with a scenario. Imagine that you and your family are very poor and cannot feed yourselves. You see a large grocery store, and you know that about 10% of their food goes to waste every day; with one of the quickest perishing items being the bread. So, the idea comes into your head to steal a loaf of bread in order to feed your family. You reason that the loaf you were going to steal likely would've been thrown away anyway. Should you steal the bread?

Let's deal with three different ways of answering this ethical question. The first way is to answer according to conscience. Some will say that as long as you do not feel that you acted wrongly, and you can perform the action according to faith, then you're free to do it. They may even site Romans 14:22-23 to back up their case.

The second way is to answer according to Scripture. The Bible says many times, "You shall not steal."[268] 1 Corinthians reminds us that thieves "will not inherit the kingdom of God."[269] Theft in general goes against the golden rule of treating others as yourself; this applies to large companies just as much as it does individuals.

The third way to answer this dilemma is to use pragmatism. Pragmatism is focused on the outcome. Through reason and understanding, pragmatism would encourage you to look at all the different outcomes and scenarios and choose the solution to the problem with the greatest positive results and least negative results.

So, which of these ethical constructs are correct? How should you, as a believer, proceed? Well, at the outset it is important to know that none of these three ethical ways of looking at this dilemma are inherently evil or morally bad. In other words, all three ethical constructs do have their place. Pragmatism (third way), dogmatism (second way) and conscience are all worthy tools in our decision making tool belt.

However, as someone who knows the reality of God and the Truth of His Word; surely what the Bible says takes supreme precedent. You are to be diligent to present yourself approved before God by "accurately handling the word of truth."[270]

In Psalm 119, the Bible is described like this: "Your word is a lamp to my feet and a light to my path."[271] In other words, Scripture is the tool that God has given us to help us guide our way through day-to-day life. As we walk along the path of our life throughout each day, it is Scripture which God uses to illuminate that path so that we do not stumble.

---

[268] Exodus 20:15; Leviticus 19:11; Matthew 19:18
[269] 1 Corinthians 6:10
[270] 2 Timothy 2:15 (NASB)
[271] Psalm 119:105 (NASB)

So, of the three ways of making ethical choices, which one takes precedence, or, is the most important? Dogmatism based upon the revealed Word of God is the ultimate way of determining God's will. As a believer, you are to be familiar with God's Word and what it says, and you are to live according to God's Word. Remember that you are to be an imitator of Jesus Christ[272], and He kept all that was written.[273] When it comes to an action with clearly revealed verses, then the believer cannot simply ignore those verses and make a claim about conscience or make an appeal to pragmatism.

Therefore, when it comes to our theft example, are you justified to steal the bread? No. Theft is always wrong and out of accord with God's Word.

Let's invert this scenario. You own a large grocery store. You catch someone stealing from you in order to feed their family. You see that they are in a desperate situation, and were only stealing for survival. What do you do?

Jesus' Sermon on the Mount clearly sets the precedent for a loving heart, and clearly says to give to those who ask, even to those who take unfairly.[274] However, it is also not an immoral thing to seek justice in a situation like this.[275] Ultimately, this scenario and situations like it come down to issues of conscience.

In this particular scenario, the overwhelming weight of Scripture and conscience would likely both err towards extreme leniency. In fact, it may well be argued that you, as the owner, should give this man a great deal more than what he sought to steal.

---

[272] 1 Peter 2:21
[273] Matthew 5:17
[274] Matthew 5; specifically relevant here are verses 38-42
[275] Proverbs 21:15

The reality is that you, as a believer, are to conduct yourself according to all three moral schemas examined. You are to live according to Scripture; which is the ultimate authority and trumps the other two. Secondly, on areas where Scripture turns over authority to the conscience, you are to lean upon the leadings of the Holy Spirit upon your conscience. Thirdly, only after an issue passes your Scriptural and conscience check, you are to examine a situation pragmatically by logically working out the expected outcomes and judging the merits of each accordingly.

By using this decision-making schema, you can determine God's will for your life in any situation:

- What does Scripture say about this topic? If it is permissible by Scripture, then proceed to the next test.
- Pray for guidance on an issue, and pay attention to your conscience. If you can make this decision happily and openly in good faith, then proceed to the next test.
- Once those tests are passed, seek the council of other believers and use logic and reason to determine the best possible solution.

Remember this ethical framework and use it for every major decision.

Practicum

Did you ever wonder why God put the tree of knowledge in the Garden if He did not want Adam to eat it? Well, the answer is simple. The Grand Narrative of all of redemptive history is all about the glory of God. The reality is that a creature that chooses to obey is more glorifying that one that has no means of disobeying.

You may be thinking to yourself, "Yeah, sure, but still why something so random and innocent as eating from a particular tree."

Well, that is exactly the point. Eating a particular tree is not inherently good or bad unless God says that it is. Remember that Adam bore the responsibility of a full image bearer of God. If Adam had lied, cheated, stolen, etc., then this too would have been a disobedient and rebellious act against our Creator.

However, God did not have to forbid these things explicitly to Adam. Why? Well, the simple fact is that Adam would not have lied, cheated, stolen, etc. because he had no desire to in his nature. Adam was created good and had no evil desires in and of himself. The only kind of evil that Adam and Eve had to contend with was external evil; spiritual evil influences upon them.

It is not an act of obedience if a rabbit prefers eating carrots instead of meat; rabbits naturally eat vegetables. Likewise, it is not an act of obedience for Adam not to lie; it is simply not in his nature. Therefore, something had to be forbidden that was completely outside of moral right and wrong. Something had to be forbidden because God declared it to be so.

You and I are in a different situation. We are of a fallen nature prior to being born again, and even after being born again we continue to struggle against our fallen flesh. We are on a much more crowded battlefield. We struggle against our flesh, we struggle against the evil within others, and we, like Adam, struggle against spiritual evil forces.

Our Lord has not left us unprepared for this battlefield, however. We have been provided a full armor:
> Put on the full armor of God, so that you will be able to stand firm against the schemes of the devil... Therefore, take up the full armor of God, so that you will be able to resist in the evil day, and having done everything, to stand firm. Stand firm therefore, having girded your loins with truth, and having put on the breastplate of righteousness, and having shod your feet with the

preparation of the gospel of peace; in addition to all, taking up the shield of faith with which you will be able to extinguish all the flaming arrows of the evil one. And take the helmet of salvation, and the sword of the Spirit, which is the word of God. With all prayer and petition pray at all times in the Spirit...[276]

First, Paul tells us to "gird our loins with truth". This is commonly referred to as the belt of Truth. The belt is that upon which your other instruments are secured. This is why science and knowledge are friends of the Christian faith, not foes. If you attempt to do battle against an enemy using falsehood, then you have already lost because the Christian Soldier is to remain in Truth at all times. Do not repeat something or make up something purely because you hope it's true; test all things and hold fast to that which is True.[277]

Second, Paul tells us to put on the breastplate of righteousness. This is not merely a reference to the righteousness of Christ which is imputed to the believer, as that is more akin to the helmet of salvation. No, in context, Paul here is indeed talking about your individual righteousness. As you engage with sin, you leave your heart unguarded. Indeed, if you sin without remorse and do not seek sanctification, then you have no reason to think of yourself as being saved.[278] The enemy will use your unrighteousness to bring you down; therefore, act righteously.

Next, we are told to put on the Gospel shoes. It is the Gospel, which is the power of God unto salvation,[279] that moves us to act and interact with others. It is the glorious Good News that is what allows us to stand firm when we battle. It is the Gospel that motivates us to

---

[276] Ephesians 6:11-18 (NASB)

[277] A paraphrase of 1 Thessalonians 5:21

[278] The inverse of 1 John 5; sanctification is how we know we are saved, therefore it flows logically that a lack of sanctification is an indication that we are not. James 2:24 carries the same message.

[279] Romans 1:16

move forward in battle, and it is our love for those that need the Good News that emboldens us.

Now to the shield of faith; there are times when you will be knocked back by an enemy offensive whether it is a personal tragedy in your life, an objection raised by someone outside the faith, an unkind or wrong action by someone inside the faith, a personal objection that's arisen, etc. When those flaming arrows come, it is important to use the shield of faith to quench the fire. A shield is exactly that, it protects you from what would otherwise be a fatal blow. You may not immediately understand a situation, or know the answer to the question, but the shield of faith will protect you as you walk through and reconcile the answer.

It goes without saying that the helmet protects the head. Paul, under inspiration of the Holy Spirit, tells us that our head is protected with the helmet of salvation. Your enemies want you to question the Word of God, in particular they want you to begin to question your own salvation. You are not worthy of the Kingdom of God, and the enemy knows that you are aware of that fact, and he will use that against you. Especially when you do stumble or fall and commit a sin that you actively wrestle against, that is when the enemy will begin to cause you to question everything. Do not let this happen. Remember at all times that you are saved by the righteousness of Christ, not your own righteousness. Remember that the natural man does not struggle with sin, but rather the unsaved person sins without remorse. The fact that you are struggling with your sin is actually a sign that you are saved. You are not to sin, and as a born again believer; you will not want to. Nevertheless, be especially on guard when you do, because that moment of weakness will be exploited by your enemy. Put on the helmet of salvation, resting securely in the fact that it is because of Jesus and Cross that you are saved. You are not good enough for the Kingdom of Heaven, but that did not stop our amazing savior from saving you anyway.

Your offensive weapon is the sword of the Spirit, which is the Bible. The particular type of sword in view here is one that is both offensive and defensive. The Gospels record our Lord wielding this weapon perfectly as He was tempted in the wilderness.[280] To use it effectively, just like with using any weapon, requires practice. If you are not spending time in the Word, or if you do not understand the Word of God, then you are not going to be effective at thwarting your enemies. It is imperative that you understand how to read Scripture, and it is equally important that you have Scripture internalized in order to be an effective soldier in battle. Imagine if the first time a Roman soldier ever lifted up a sword was when he was sent to the front lines... is it likely that he is going to be very effective or is it more likely that he is going to be destroyed?

Last but not least we are told to pray at all times. Prayer is an essential part of your life here in this world; in this age. Jesus Himself modeled a prayerful life for us, and it is essential that we do the same. Our Lord exhorts His disciples saying, "You do not have because you do not ask. You ask and do not receive, because you ask with wrong motives, so that you may spend it on your pleasures."[281] Oftentimes, we lack because we have not turned a situation over to God in prayer. At other times we lack because, although we have turned it over to God in prayer, we have done so with selfish motives.

The guidelines for our prayer life are the same as with every other aspect of our lives. We should be in constant communion with God. And with prayer, just as with all things, our motives for asking should be ultimately seeking the glory of God and/or the love of our neighbor.

Unlike Adam, you face many battlefronts as a believer in this present age. However, your enemy is never another person or people group. No, your enemy is your own flesh and the dark spiritual forces

---

[280] Matthew 4:1-11; Mark 1:12-13; Luke 4:1-13
[281] John 4:2-3 (NASB)

against you in the world. If you securely wear the belt of truth, wear an unblemished breastplate of righteousness, move forward and stand firm in the Gospel shoes, quench the fire of the enemy with your shield of faith, firmly fasten the helmet of salvation, rightly wield the sword of the Spirit and pray in all things, then you will be a victorious and great soldier in the Lord's Army.

Join the battle!

ACKNOWLEDGEMENTS

This book would not have been possible without the work and input of several individuals.

This book is a fruit of the Lord's Army Ministry. That is a ministry that was birthed out of the amazing bible studies that took place under Brian McDonald at a Waffle House. His insight and input run throughout this work. Likewise, a special thanks to my friend and mentor, Dr. Mark Spellman, who has been forced to suffer through more of my writings than anyone else on this earth. His guidance and instruction have grown me significantly over the years.

This literal book itself would not have come about if not for the advice and encouragement of Michael Rowand. Not only do his teachings regularly bless and encourage me, but also he was the one who helped me realize that I had already written a book and did not even know it.

Finally, if this book was enjoyable to read at all, then it must be acknowledged that this is owed in large part to Abbie Lutz. As the editor of this book, she is the one who spent a great deal of time and ink identifying my propensity for repetitious word choices, run-on sentences and nonsensical ramblings.